Southern Africa's Mammals

a field guide

Southern Africa's Mammals

a field guide

ROBIN FRANDSEN

FRANDSEN PUBLISHERS
Sandton
1992

First impression 1992
Second impression 1993
Third impression 1994
Fourth impression 1994
Fifth impression 1995
Sixth impression 1995

Published in South Africa by:
Frandsen Publishers (Pty) Ltd
P O Box 122, Fourways 2055

© Robin Frandsen

Editor – Joy Frandsen
Reproduction and typesetting by Pointset (Pty) Ltd, Randburg
Printed and bound by National Book Printers, Drukkery Street, Goodwood, Western Cape
Design, all black and white illustrations and maps are by the author
Front cover – Leopard, photograph Anup Shah/ABPL
Title page – Etosha scene, photograph David Frandsen
Back cover – Brown hyaena, Anthony Bannister/ABPL

ISBN 0-9583124-5-1

Hierdie boek is ook beskikbaar in Afrikaans onder die titel *Suider-Afrika se Soogdiere*

Dieses Buch ist auch verfügbar in Deutsch mit dem titel *Säugetiere des Südlichen Afrika*

To Joy,
Jeffrey, David, Elizabeth
and Vincent

Acknowledgements

I would like to thank the following persons who have willingly contributed their assistance, advice and knowledge: Dr S C J Joubert, who also wrote the foreword, Dr I L Rautenbach, Gary Bronner, Lorna Stanton, Petri Viljoen, Howard Geach and Mike Norris.

Special thanks to Nico and Ella Myburgh for their continued friendship and encouragement.

To my friend Dieter Mandlmeier I would like to express a special thank you for his valuable professional advice, which has made the book so attractive.

Thanks go to all the photographers who provided the photographs, without which the book could not be a success, with special mention of Tony Bannister and his staff.

My heartfelt thanks to my wife Joy for her patient editing and correction of the manuscript, and to my son David for his helpful and valuable suggestions, all of which helped to bring the book to fruition.

Most of all my praise and thanks to my Creator, Who has made the wonderful creatures which are the subject of this book. All the glory goes to Him.

Robin Frandsen
Sandton
1992

Foreword

In the course of the past two decades two extremely important trends have manifested themselves in the field of nature conservation. On the one hand, a discernible awareness of the environment has become apparent amongst the people of South Africa; and on the other, a proliferation of natural history books has complemented this rapidly growing awareness. Both trends are to be welcomed.

Southern Africa is endowed with a particularly rich diversity of mammal species, and should this natural heritage be preserved for the benefit of our future generations it is vitally important that the habitats they occupy should also remain intact. Man, however, has also a legitimate claim to develop and manage the natural resources for his own benefit and qualities of life. To achieve a rational balance between the preservation of pristine ecosystems, with all their intriguing attributes, and the sustainable utilization of natural resources to support human populations, is the objective towards which all responsible citizens should strive.

To meet this challenge, an intimate knowledge of all aspects of our natural environment is a prerequisite. In this respect, our comprehensive collection of natural history books, and the variety of formats in which they have been presented to meet the needs of different segments of our society, has played a major rôle. The latest addition to this collection, Robin Frandsen's book on the mammals of southern Africa must, in itself, also be valued as a major contribution towards a better knowledge of, and a deeper insight into, our rich mammal fauna. It not only contains a wealth of information, but in the structuring of the text Robin Frandsen has also succeeded in making it readily accessible to all users, in a most skilful manner. Together with distribution maps, superb photographs and line drawings, and an easy-to-use key for the rapid identification of the major mammal families, this latest edition, 'Southern Africa's Mammals' meets, in every respect, the demands of a field guide in the true sense of the word.

This is a book which deserves its rightful place in the rucksacks of trailists, the front seats of cars touring through our nature reserves and on the bookshelves of all true nature lovers. I have no doubt that this book will generously contribute to the broadening of our knowledge of our natural environment, to the creation of an even greater awareness and appreciation of our mammals - both large and small - and the promotion of an environmental ethic. I wish it every success in meeting these high ideals!

DR S C J JOUBERT
Executive Director: Kruger National Park

Contents

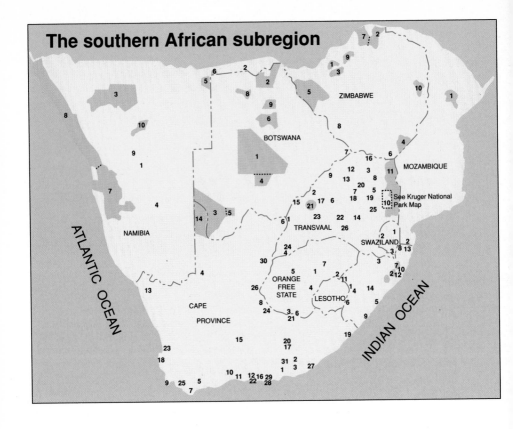

The southern African subregion

GAME RESERVES AND NATIONAL PARKS

TRANSVAAL

 1 *Barberspan* - W. Transvaal
 2 *Ben Alberts* - N.W. Transvaal
 3 *Ben Lavin* - N. Transvaal
 4 *Bloemhof Dam* - S.W. Transvaal
 5 *Blyde River Canyon* - E. Transvaal
 6 *Borokolano* - central Transvaal
 7 *Doorndraai Dam* - N. Transvaal
 8 *Hans Merensky* - N. Transvaal
 9 *Hans Strydom Dam* - N. Transvaal
10 *Klaserie* - E. Transvaal
11 *Kruger Park* - E. Transvaal
12 *Langjan* - N. Transvaal
13 *Lapalala* - N. Transvaal
10 *Londolozi* - E. Transvaal
14 *Loskop Dam* - E. Transvaal
15 *Madikwe* - W. Transvaal

10 *Mala Mala* - E. Transvaal
10 *Manyeleti* - E. Transvaal
16 *Messina* - N. Transvaal
17 *Nyala Ranch* - W. Transvaal
18 *Nylsvley* - N. Transvaal
19 *Orighstad Dam* - E. Transvaal
20 *Percy Fyfe* - N. Transvaal
21 *Pilanesberg* - W. Transvaal
22 *Roodeplaat Dam* - Pretoria
23 *Rustenburg* - W. Transvaal
10 *Sabi-Sabi* - E. Transvaal
10 *Sabi Sand* - E. Transvaal
24 *S A Lombard* - S.W. Transvaal
25 *Sterkspruit* - E. Transvaal
26 *Suikerbosrand* - S. Transvaal
10 *Thornybush* - E. Transvaal
10 *Timbavati* - E. Transvaal

10 *Umbabat/Motswari* - E. Transvaal

NATAL
1 *Giants Castle* - Natal Midlands
2 *Hluhluwe/Umfolozi Park* - Zululand
3 *Itala* - N. Natal
4 *Kamberg* - Natal Midlands
5 *Kenneth Stainbank* - Durban
6 *Loteni* - Drakensberg
7 *Mkuzi* - Zululand
8 *Ndumu* - Zululand
9 *Oribi Gorge* - S. Natal
10 *Phinda* - Zululand
11 *Royal Natal* - Drakensberg
12 *St Lucia* - Zululand
13 *Tembe Elephant* - N. Zululand
14 *Weenen* - Natal Midlands

ORANGE FREE STATE
1 *Erfenis Dam* - central O.F.S.
2 *Golden Gate* - E. O.F.S.
3 *Hendrik Verwoerd Dam* - S. O.F.S.
4 *Maria Maroka* - central O.F.S.
5 *Soetdoring* - central O.F.S.
6 *Tussen-die-riviere* - S. O.F.S.
7 *Willem Pretorius* - central O.F.S.

CAPE PROVINCE
1 *Addo Elephant Park* - E. Cape
2 *Amalinda* - E. Cape
3 *Andries Vosloo* - E. Cape
4 *Aughrabies* - N. Cape
5 *Bontebok* - S.W. Cape
6 *Botsalano* - N. Cape
7 *De Hoop* - S. Cape
8 *Doornkloof* - N. Great Karoo
9 *Cape Point* - S.W. Cape
10 *Gamkaberg* - S. Cape
11 *Gamkapoort* - S. Cape
12 *Goukamma* - S. Cape
13 *Hester Malan* - N.W. Cape
14 *Kalahari Gemsbok* - N. Cape
15 *Karoo* - central Great Karoo
16 *Keurboom* - S. Cape
17 *Kommando Drift* - E. Cape
18 *Langebaan* - S.W. Cape
19 *Mkambati* - N.E. Cape
20 *Mountain Zebra* - E. Cape
21 *Oviston* - N. Great Karoo
22 *Robberg* - S. Cape
23 *Rocher Pan* - S.W. Cape

24 *Rolfontein* - N. Great Karoo
25 *Salmon's Dam* - S.W. Cape
26 *Sandveld* - N. Great Karoo
27 *Thomas Baines* - E. Cape
28 *Tsitsikama Coast* - S. Cape
29 *Tsitsikama Forest* - S. Cape
30 *Vaalbos* - N.E. Cape
31 *Zuurberg* - E. Cape

SWAZILAND
1 *Hlane* - N.E. Swaziland
2 *Mlilwane* - W. Swaziland
3 *Pongolo* - S. Swaziland

NAMIBIA
1 *Daan Viljoen* - central Namibia
2 *E.& W. Caprivi* - N.E. Namibia
3 *Etosha* - N. Namibia
4 *Hardap* - central Namibia
5 *Khaudom* - N.E. Namibia
6 *Mahango* - W. Caprivi
7 *Naukluft* - W. Namibia
8 *Skeleton Coast* - N.W. Namibia
9 *Von Bach* - N. central Namibia
10 *Waterberg Plateau* - central Namibia

BOTSWANA
1 *Central Kalahari* - central Botswana
2 *Chobe* - N. Botswana
3 *Gemsbok* - S.W. Botswana
4 *Khutse* - S. central Botswana
5 *Mabuasehube* - S.W. Botswana
6 *Makghadikgadi Pan* - central Botswana
7 *Mashatu* - E. Botswana
8 *Moremi* - N. Botswana
9 *Nxai Pan* - N. central Botswana

ZIMBABWE
1 *Chete* - N.W. Zimbabwe
2 *Chewore* - N. Zimbabwe
3 *Chizarira* - N.W. Zimbabwe
4 *Gonarhezhou* - E. Zimbabwe
5 *Hwange* - W. Zimbabwe
6 *Malapati* - E. Zimbabwe
7 *Mana Pools* - N. Zimbabwe
8 *Matopos* - W. Zimbabwe
9 *Matusadona* - N. Zimbabwe
10 *Nyanga* - E. Zimbabwe

MOZAMBIQUE
1 *Gorongosa* - N.E. Mozambique
2 *Maputo Elephant* - S. Mozambique

Introduction

The first and foremost purpose of a field guide on mammals is to provide a rapid identification of the animals when they are encountered in habitat. I have set out with the express intention of addressing this need and readers, even with little knowledge of the subject, should be able to rapidly find their way in the book to the animal which they have seen in the wild, and identify it. This will add inestimably to the reader's enjoyment of game viewing.

This book deals with the scope of what readers need and want in a field guide. It is specifically designed to provide rapid identification and in-depth information on all land mammals from hedgehog-size upwards. Although a great deal of information is included, the sections are so structured as to avoid a cluttered effect. Each section is clearly divided - the illustrations, distribution maps, spoors and vital information on one page, adjacent to the relative text.

For even more in-depth study of all the mammals of the sub-region, several excellent and definitive books, such as Reay H.N. Smithers' *The Mammals of the Southern African Subregion*, are available which will give complete and scientific insight into the subject. That depth of study is out of the scope of a field guide.

In preparing this manuscript, I have avoided the format wherein the obvious features of the animals are dealt with in a repetitive form. For the sake of brevity, any description which is not necessary for identification and which is obvious from the illustration is not included. Readers usually know that an elephant is large and grey, has a trunk at one end and a tail at the other, and do not need to be told that. What have been included, however, are the morphological and fascinating behavioral facts of the animals which are not obvious, and which will make finding and identifying each animal so much more enjoyable and interesting.

I have tried to present the fascinating, and sometimes hidden, facts in a readable and interesting, informal format, and also to portray clearly the diagnostic identification details in the illustrations. The user will be able to enjoy rapidly identifying the animals with which this guide deals, as well as gaining greater insight into and knowledge of southern Africa's wildlife.

Contents: The contents pages give the taxonomic sections of the animals. This includes the classifications of family, sub-family, group and subgroup.

Rapid Identification Guide: This unique method of illustrated identification is to assist the reader in very rapid identification of the animal. The number, or numbers, listed are those numbers allocated to the animal in the guide and similarly in the main text and do NOT refer to page numbers.

When an animal which has been sighted is to be identified, a rapid glance through the illustrations in the 'Rapid Identification Guide' section of the book should take the reader immediately to the correct grouping of animals. A short line on some of the illustrations points to a specific obvious feature to further aid in rapid identification. The numbering of that group of animals then enables the reader to turn to the section with similar numbering in the main text and to thus quickly identify the animal which has been seen.

Further aid for identification is the measurement following the number and name, which is either of the animal's average shoulder height or total length.

For the sake of clarity and brevity, not all the animals are individually illustrated in this 'rapid identification guide' section of the book. When the animals are similar, then only one representative of the group is given as a guide to that group. If any of the group are so radically different as to make comparative identification difficult, then that animal is illustrated individually.

Illustrations: Usually one clear diagnostic photograph is reproduced to show the animal. On the same page are the hind and fore spoors. A table of statistics is included, in which the measurements recorded are average figures and the longevity is usually established from animals in captivity. Animals in the wild usually live shorter and more precarious lives.

Text: The text on the relative animal appears adjacent to the illustrations. Where there is a group of animals within a section, for example the Hyaenidae (aardwolf, spotted hyaena and brown hyaena), all these animals are grouped, together with a short introductory paragraph, so that their relationship is understood and a clear comparison of their diversities is easily seen.

Maps and distribution: There is a colour map of the southern African sub-region indicating the location of the various parks and reserves, as well as one of the Kruger National Park and another of the northern Natal conservation areas.

Two types of distribution maps are included. On the page with the illustration of each animal is a distribution map of southern Africa, in which the range of the particular animal is recorded. If the animal is recorded as occurring in the Kruger National Park, then a map of the park is also included, on the text page, giving the distribution within the park boundaries.

The relevant distribution lists, at the end of each section of text on every animal, record the national parks and reserves throughout southern Africa in which the animals are to be found.

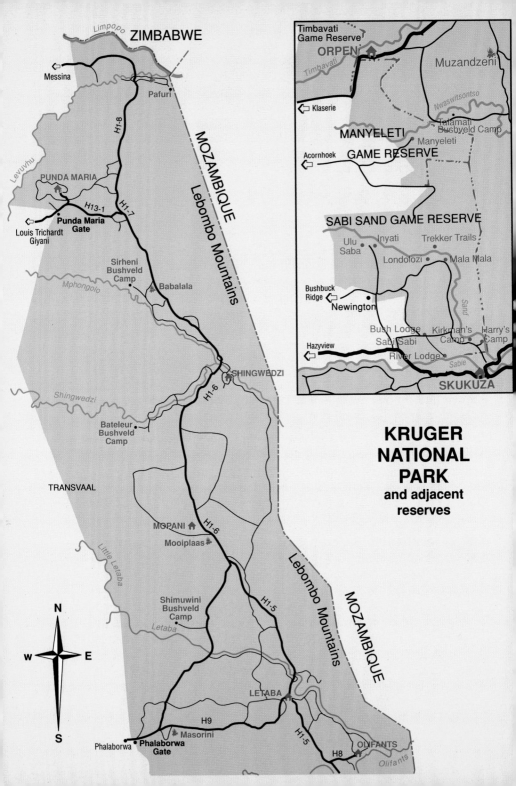

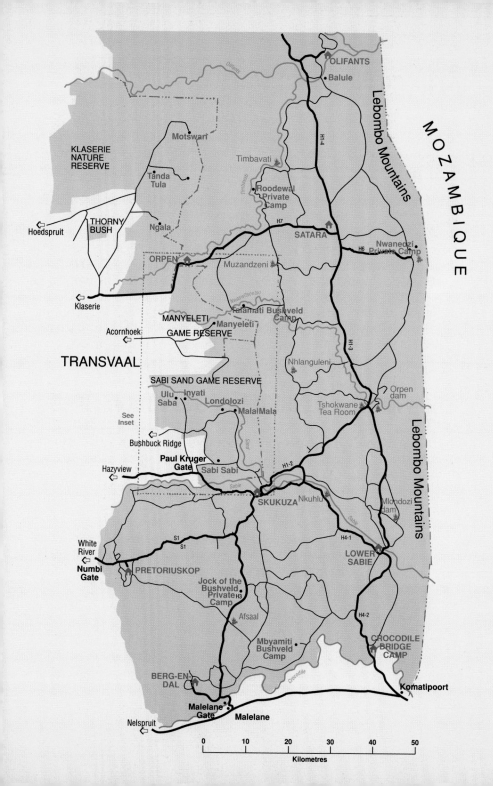

Kruger National Park

The most visited reserve and conservation area in the subregion is the Kruger National Park. Internationally renowned, it is the holiday destination for many thousands of local visitors, as well as for visitors from all over the world. Special features relating to the park are included in this book to make their visit informative and enjoyable.

Many factors influence the varying occurrence of animals throughout the park. The concentration of animals, or indeed their very presence or absence, is dictated by these factors. The Kruger Park map, included with the text on each animal that occurs in the Park, shows the degree of possibility of seeing the animal in the area through which the visitor is travelling.

Unshaded areas indicate where it is unlikely that the animal will be seen. Shading is used to show areas where there is a probable occurrence and darker shading shows where there is the greatest likelihood of a sighting. However, neither light nor dark shading is an indication of abundance or rarity of the animal. This is indicated by the caption below the map.

The Northern Natal Conservation Areas

Much land in northern Natal has been set aside for the conservation of the very diverse ecosystems of the region. Several of these areas, like the Hluhluwe, Umfolozi, St Lucia (with its extensive wetlands), Mkuze, Itala and Ndumo reserves are internationally famous. The responsible authorities have created fine facilities within these reserves for lovers of nature to enjoy viewing the remarkable diversity of the animal, bird and plant life.

In addition to the game reserves there are the various coastal reserves, such as the Sodwana National Park which, with its rich tropical marine reefs, is the mecca for scuba divers. Other important coastal reserves are the St Lucia Marine Reserve, Kosi Bay Nature Reserve and the Maputaland Marine Sanctuary.

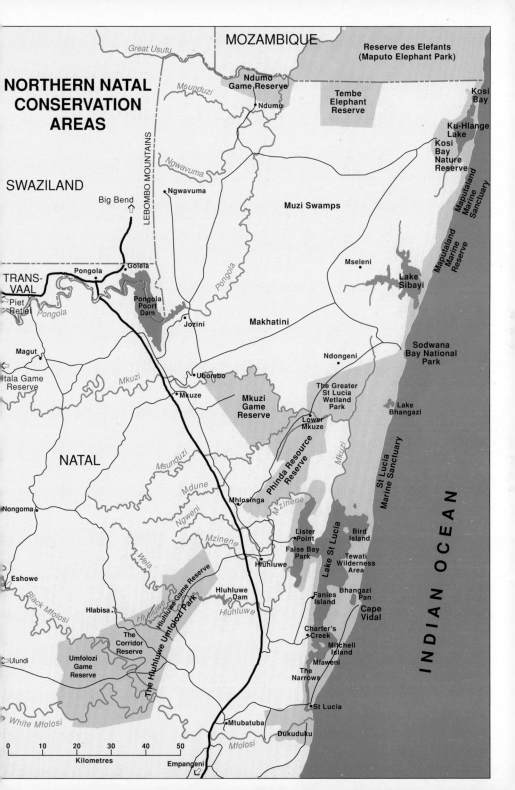

Rapid Identification Guide

The following pages give you a concise rapid visual reference to the animal you may have sighted. When you find the animal refer quickly to the same number, in the main text of the book, for all the interesting details which should verify the identification. If that number should not be the animal sought then a quick glance to the colour photographs immediately preceding or immediately following, will be sure to take you to the animal sought.

1 HEDGEHOG

South African hedgehog

Length: 19 cm

2-3 BUSHBABY

2 Thick-tailed bushbaby
Length: 55 cm
3 Lesser bushbaby
Length: 35 cm

*Thick-tailed
bushbaby*

4 BABOON

Chacma baboon

Length: 1,2 m

5-6 MONKEY

5 Vervet monkey
Length: 1,1 m
6 Samango monkey
Length: 1,3 m

*Vervet
monkey*

7 PANGOLIN

Length: 80 cm

8-10 HARE & RABBIT

8 Cape hare
Length: 55 cm
9 Scrub hare
Length: 55 cm
10 Riverine rabbit
Length: 43 cm

Scrub hare

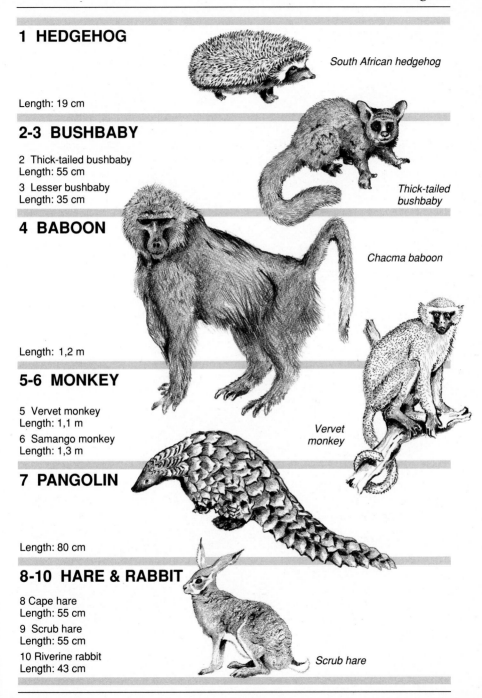

11 PORCUPINE

Length: 75 cm

12 SPRINGHAAS

Length: 80 cm

13-14 SQUIRREL

13 Ground squirrel
Length: 46 cm

14 Tree squirrel
Length: 35 cm

Ground squirrel

15 AARDWOLF

Length: 90 cm

16-17 HYAENA

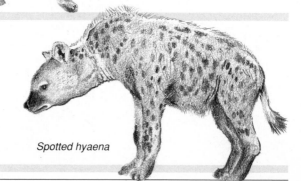

16 Spotted hyaena
Shoulder height: 85 cm

17 Brown hyaena
Shoulder height: 79 cm

Spotted hyaena

18 LION

Length: 2,6 m

19 LEOPARD

Length: 2 m

20 CHEETAH

Length: 2 m

21 CARACAL

Length: 1,1 m

22 SERVAL

Length: 1,1 m

23-24 CAT

23 Small-spotted cat
Length: 58 cm

24 African wild cat
Length: 90 cm

African wild cat

25 & 27 FOX

Bat-eared fox

25 Bat-eared fox
Length: 80 cm

27 Cape fox
Length: 90 cm

Cape fox

26 WILD DOG

Shoulder height: 68 cm

28-29 JACKAL

28 Black-backed jackal
Length: 1,1 m

29 Side-striped jackal
Length: 1,1 m

Black-backed jackal

30 OTTER

Length: 1,3 m

Cape clawless otter

31 BADGER

Honey badger

Length: 95 cm

32 POLECAT

Striped polecat

Length: 60 cm

33-34 GENET

33 Small-spotted genet
Length: 95 cm

34 Large-spotted genet
Length: 1 m

Small-spotted genet

35 CIVET

African civet

Length: 1,3 m

37-42 MONGOOSE

37 Yellow mongoose
Length: 58 cm
38 Slender mongoose
Length: 60 cm
39 White-tailed mongoose
Length: 1,1 m
40 Water mongoose
Length: 90 cm
41 Banded mongoose
Length: 58 cm
42 Dwarf mongoose
Length: 38 cm

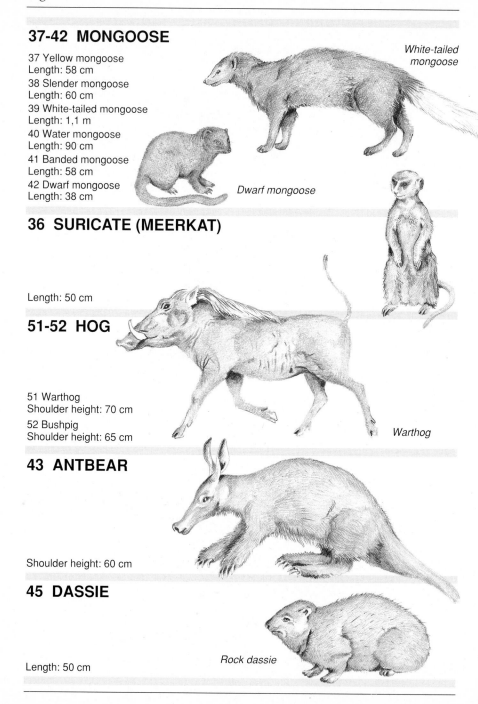

White-tailed mongoose

Dwarf mongoose

36 SURICATE (MEERKAT)

Length: 50 cm

51-52 HOG

51 Warthog
Shoulder height: 70 cm
52 Bushpig
Shoulder height: 65 cm

Warthog

43 ANTBEAR

Shoulder height: 60 cm

45 DASSIE

Length: 50 cm

Rock dassie

44 ELEPHANT

Shoulder height: 2,8

46-47 RHINOCEROS

*White
rhinoceros*

46 White rhinoceros
Shoulder height: 1,8 m

47 Black rhinoceros
Shoulder height: 1,6 m

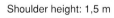

53 HIPPOPOTAMUS

Shoulder height: 1,5 m

54 GIRAFFE

Shoulder height: 3,3 m

48-50 ZEBRA

48 Burchell's zebra
Shoulder height: 1,5 m
49 Cape mountain zebra
Shoulder height: 1,25 m
50 Hartmann's mountain zebra
Shoulder height: 1,5 m

Burchell's zebra

55-56 WILDEBEEST

55 Black wildebeest
Shoulder height: 1,2 m
56 Blue Wildebeest
Shoulder height: 1,5 m

Blue wildebeest

57 HARTEBEEST

Red hartebeest

Shoulder height: 1,35 m

58-59 BONTEBOK & BLESBOK

58 Bontebok
Shoulder height: 90 cm
59 Blesbok
Shoulder height: 95 cm

Bontebok

60 TSESSEBE

Shoulder height: 1,2 m

61-63 DUIKER

61 Common duiker
Shoulder height: 50 cm
62 Red duiker
Shoulder height: 43 cm
63 Blue duiker
Shoulder height: 30 cm

Common duiker

64 SPRINGBOK

Shoulder height: 75 cm

65 KLIPSPRINGER

Shoulder height: 55 cm

66 DIK-DIK

Damara dik-dik

Shoulder height: 38 cm

67-68 ORIBI & STEENBOK

67 Oribi
Shoulder height: 58 cm

68 Steenbok
Shoulder height: 50 cm

Oribi

Steenbok

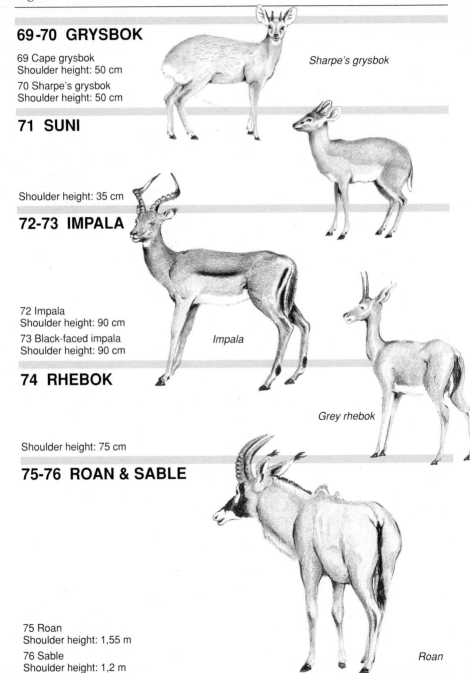

69-70 GRYSBOK

69 Cape grysbok
Shoulder height: 50 cm

70 Sharpe's grysbok
Shoulder height: 50 cm

Sharpe's grysbok

71 SUNI

Shoulder height: 35 cm

72-73 IMPALA

72 Impala
Shoulder height: 90 cm

73 Black-faced impala
Shoulder height: 90 cm

Impala

74 RHEBOK

Grey rhebok

Shoulder height: 75 cm

75-76 ROAN & SABLE

75 Roan
Shoulder height: 1,55 m

76 Sable
Shoulder height: 1,2 m

Roan

77 GEMSBOK

Shoulder height: 1,2 m

78 BUFFALO

Shoulder height: 1,6 m

79 KUDU

Shoulder height: 1,5 m

80 SITATUNGA

Shoulder height: 1,2 m

81 NYALA

Shoulder height: 1,1 m

82 BUSHBUCK

Shoulder height: 80 cm

83 ELAND

Shoulder height: 1,7 m

84-85 REEDBUCK

84 Reedbuck
Shoulder height: 90 cm

85 Mountain reedbuck
Shoulder height: 73 cm

Reedbuck

86 WATERBUCK

Shoulder height: 1,7 cm

87-88 LECHWE & PUKU

87 Red Lechwe
Shoulder height: 1 m

88 Puku
Shoulder height: 80 cm

Red lechwe

South African hedgehog

Atelerix frontalis

Krimpvarkie

There are several different species of hedgehog in Africa, Europe and Asia, but only one in southern Africa.

These tiny animals, which weigh up to 400 grammes, adapt to many different environments. They are equally at home in suburbia, semi-arid veld, grasslands or shrublands. They tend to avoid forested areas and wet ground and are absent from areas of high rainfall and the coastal desert of Namibia.

They are usually nocturnal but will venture out in the daytime after rains, probably to take advantage of surfaced earthworms and flying insects. During the day they rest under matted undergrowth, bushes or in holes. Their favourite resting place in gardens is under piles of garden refuse. These places are changed daily except when they are bearing young, at which time the female will remain at the same place until the young are able to accompany her.

When they encounter others of their kind their voice is a snuffling, snorting and growling, and is accompanied by much butting. The alarm cry is a high-pitched scream as if in pain.

Before winter, hedgehogs fatten with increased food intake. During cold periods they enter a state of semi-hibernation, which is not as profound as with some other animals. In unseasonable rains or warmer periods the sleepy animals could venture out. They may even eat a little, but not with the gusto of their usual summer feeding.

Defence consists of rolling into a ball, with the head, softer underparts, legs and tail secure within a ball of erect hard and sharp prickles. This defence system is adequate in most cases, even from the unwanted attentions of a lion. The scaly, and strong taloned feet of the giant eagle owl or spotted eagle owl, however, make short work of this defence.

One to nine, more usually about four, flattish, oval, blind and naked young are born in a well-hidden, sheltered nest. The tips of white spines just show through the skin. These are shed between a month and six weeks and replaced with the adult darker spines. The eyes open in about fourteen days and at about six weeks they are ready to forage with their mother.

Food: Hedgehogs are omnivorous, with their main food being insects. Even the millipede is taken despite its noxious secretion. Small mice,

HEDGEHOG
Gestation period: ± 35 days
Young: one – nine (usually four)
Mass: 400 g.
Length: 19 cm.
Life expectancy: 3 years

Right fore

Right hind

Actual size

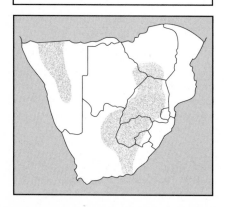

lizards, bird nestlings, eggs, vegetable matter and fungi form part of the diet. In captivity they will tolerate a wide variety of food. They are not dependent on water, absorbing all the moisture needed from their food. They will, however, drink if water is available. Although their eyesight is poor, their sense of smell is acute and hearing good, which helps them detect prey, even though it is underground.

Very rare

Distribution: SOUTH AFRICA: *Transvaal*: Barberspan, Ben Alberts, Borokalano, Doorndraai Dam, Hans Strydom Dam, Kruger Park, Langjan, Lapalala, Nyala Ranch, Nylsvley, Percy Fyfe, Pilanesberg, Roodeplaat Dam, Rustenburg, S A Lombard, Suikerbosrand; *O.F.S.*: Bloemhof Dam, Golden Gate, Hendrik Verwoerd Dam, Soetdoring, Tussen-die-Riviere; *Cape*: Andries Vosloo, Botsalano, Doornkloof, Kalahari Gemsbok, Kommandodrift, Mountain Zebra, Rolfontein, Thomas Baines, Zuurberg.

NAMIBIA: Daan Viljoen, Etosha, Von Bach, Waterberg Plateau; BOTSWANA: Makgadikgadi, Nxai Pan; ZIMBABWE: Hwange, Matopos.

BUSHBABIES:

The name 'galago' was originally the native name in Senegal for these animals. It was adopted, is still in use in the northern hemisphere and it is sometimes used in the south.

A total of six species occur in the African continent, with two being found in the subregion: the lesser and the thick-tailed bushbabies. Both are small arboreal animals with large, sensitive eyes, well adapted to their nocturnal habit. The eyes are almost immobile in their sockets, compensated by very mobile heads, which are able to turn through 180°. Their expressions are fixed as they have no muscular facial movement.

Similar to the lesser bushbaby, Grant's bushbaby, *Galagoides grantii* occurs from eastern Mozambique, extending into Chimanimani in eastern Zimbabwe. They are distinguished from the lesser bushbaby by being browner overall and slightly larger. They are more gregarious, the call harsher and louder, and they are more carnivorous.

Thick-tailed bushbaby
Otolemur crassicaudatus
Bosnagaap

These bushbabies are also known as greater galagos. They are gregarious, forming stable groups of two to six individuals, resting together in the day

THICK-TAILED BUSHBABY

Gestation period: ± 130 days	
Young: one – three (usually one – two)	
Mass: ♂ 1,20 kg, ♀ 0,80 kg.	
Total Length: ♂ 60 cm, ♀ 52 cm.	
Life expectancy: 14 years	

Right front

Actual size

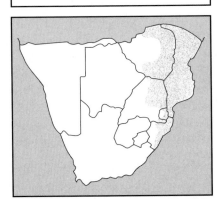

Right hind

and dispersing solitarily at night to forage along fairly established routes. Their resting places are associated with dense creepers and their habitat is thickets, forests and dense woodland. The young males show an increasing tendency to wander further and further away from their usual range, eventually establishing their own territories and eventually their own groups.

They are very agile, leaping effortlessly through the trees. On the ground, they move on their four limbs with the tail held high, rather like their cousins, the lemurs, or will hop along on their hind legs. When angry and in defence they will strike with their hands and bite viciously. Their fights are often fatal.

Though normally silent, vocalisation is a long loud wailing, repeated harshly over a long period, not unlike a child crying - hence their name. This call, which may be answered, is heard over a considerable distance. The dialogue is probably a territorial communication.

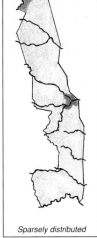

Enemies are nocturnal raptors and predators such as genet and python. One to three, usually one or two, young are born. They chitter in the nest when they are disturbed or utter a loud clicking when afraid. They are born in the usual resting nests, which have been specially lined for the occasion.

Food: Food is fruit, nuts, leaves, berries, small birds, bird's eggs, sap, insects and small reptiles. Live prey is caught by a lightning jump. Caged poultry and game birds are sometimes killed and only the heads eaten.

Distribution: SOUTH AFRICA: *Transvaal*: Klaserie, Kruger Park, Londolozi, Mala Mala, Manyeleti, Messina, Sabi-Sabi, Sabi-Sand, Timbavati, Umbabat/Motswari; *Natal*: Hluhluwe, Mkuzi, Ndumu, Oribi Gorge, Phinda, St Lucia.

Sparsely distributed

BOTSWANA: Mashatu; ZIMBABWE: Gonarhezhou, Matopos, Nyanga; MOZAMBIQUE: Gorongosa, Maputo Elephant.

Lesser bushbaby

Galago moholi

Nagapie

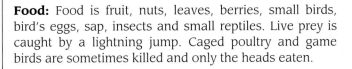

These very attractive, small woolly primates are gregarious and, like the thick-tailed bushbaby, live harmoniously together. They rest together in the day and disperse for their solitary nocturnal forage. The resting place or nest may be an old bird's nest, or a platform of sticks and grass or, in suburbia, in the hollow between roof and ceiling. They leave the nest at a fixed

LESSER BUSHBABY

Gestation period: ± 240 days	
Young: usually one, often twins	
Mass: 170 g.	
Total Length: 35 cm.	
Life expectancy: 14 years	

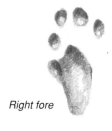

Right fore

Right hind

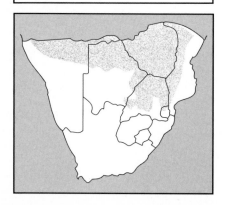

Actual size

time every evening, later in winter and earlier in summer, and it is almost possible to check one's watch against the time of their emerging. They sleep in many diverse positions, even upside down with ears folded back. If disturbed they are very languid and are loth to wake up fully.

Their vocalisation is varied, grunts and moans when eating, clicking on finding unusual objects, moaning as a warning, a 'tchak-tchak' rising to a rapid chittering if angry, or a twitter among themselves as a contact call. Young will utter a high clicking if disturbed and a soft grunting when suckling or when content.

Enemies are the same as the thick-tailed bushbaby. One or two young are born in the nest, which is usually relined for the occasion. One or two young are produced.

Uncommon, widely distributed

Food: The main food is a diet of gum, exuded from, in particular, *Acacia* trees, insects and other invertebrates. Probably eat the heads of young birds. Grant's bushbaby eats birds, small mammals, bird's eggs and fruit.

Distribution: SOUTH AFRICA: *Transvaal*: Ben Alberts, Ben Lavin, Klaserie, Kruger Park, Lapalala, Londolozi, Loskop Dam, Mala Mala, Manyeleti, Messina, Nyala Ranch, Nylsvley, Pilanesberg, Roodeplaat Dam, Rustenburg, Sabi-Sabi, Sabi-Sand, Suikerbosrand, Timbavati, Umbabat/Motswari.

NAMIBIA: Eastern & Western Caprivi, Kaudom, Mahonga; BOTSWANA: Chobe, Mashatu, Moremi; ZIMBABWE: Chete, Chizarira, Gonarhezhou, Malapati, Matopos, Matusadona, Nyanga, Hwange.

BABOONS & MONKEYS

Many baboon and monkey species are found throughout Africa but only two baboon species are found in the subregion and only the chacma baboon is dealt with, for the other, the yellow baboon (*Papio cynocephalus*), is found in the subregion only in northern Mozambique.

Two species of monkey are encountered in the subregion. The most common, the vervet, or blue monkey, is a locally common animal, which in some built-up areas has reached pest status. The samango monkey, on the other hand is a relatively rare inhabitant of forests and is not generally regarded as a problem animal.

✓ # Chacma baboon

Papio ursinus

Kaapse Bobbejaan

4

The Chacmas vary considerably in colour across their range but are generally a grizzled greyish colour. The tails, about the same length as the head and body together, are usually carried with the proximal or upper third part upright and the balance downwards. The juncture between these two sections is sharply kinked. The sexes are best distinguished by the formation of the ischial callosities on their rears. The females have their callosities in two sections, separated by the vulva which becomes swollen and red when the animal is in oestrus, and the male's callosities are in one section with the left and right hand parts joined below the anus. This is presented by the female to the male as a sexual advance and also as a social greeting.

These common, gregarious animals form troops of sometimes more than fifty individuals. The adult males may move between troops which maintain a range which they defend, usually rather peacefully, but savage fights do occur. The troops are ruled by dominant males; in small troops by a single individual and in larger troops by as many as twelve. Males sit idly at a vantage point ready to bark a warning of any danger; they also serve to protect the troop by keeping the youngsters from straying and by staying on the edges of a moving troop.

Their preferred habitat is in proximity to rocky hills and kranzes for resting at night. They also rest in tall trees. They do, however, range far and wide to forage. The voice is a bi-syllabic bark of the adult males, which is repeated intermittently. It is particularly stimulated when danger is threatened. They also grunt, and in excitement this rises to a sharp snore. 'Wah-wah' accompanied by head-rocking and tail-waving indicates great pleasure.

Right fore

Right
hind

½ actual size

CHACMA BABOON
Gestation period: ± 187 days (6 months)
Young: one, very rarely two
Mass: ♂ 27 kg, ♀ 20 kg.
Total Length: ♂ 1,2 m, ♀ 0,9m.
Life expectancy: 18 years (over 30 years in captivity)

Left fore

Left hind

³/₄ actual size

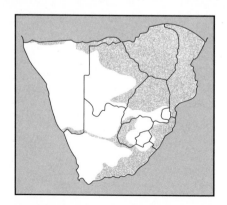

VERVET MONKEY

Gestation period: ± 200 days

Young: one, rarely twins

Mass: ♂ 5 kg, ♀ 4 kg.

Length: ♂ 110 cm, ♀ 100 cm.

Life expectancy: 12 years,
up to 24 years in captivity

They are preyed upon by the larger carnivores, but are well able to defend themselves using their long powerful canines, and are particularly dangerous in a pack. One young, very rarely twins, is produced at any time throughout the year.

Food: They are omnivorous, the main diet being vegetation and in particular, grass. They eat a wide range of fruits, seeds and plant matter. Insects and other invertebrates are taken and they relish scorpions which are lifted carefully and the sting flicked off. They hunt and kill smaller species of antelope and the young of antelope, domestic poultry and the young of goats, as well as hares and reptiles. Regular access to water is essential. Older males are not above cannibalism of the young of their own troops.

Common to very common

Distribution: SOUTH AFRICA: *Transvaal*: Ben Alberts, Borokalano, Doorndraai Dam, Hans Merensky, Hans Strydom Dam, Klaserie, Kruger Park, Langjan, Lapalala, Londolozi, Mala Mala, Manyeleti, Messina, Nyala Ranch, Nylsvley, Percy Fyfe, Pilanesberg, Rustenburg, Sabi-Sabi, Sabi-Sand, Suikerbosrand, Timbavati, Umbabat/Motswari; *O.F.S.*: Golden Gate, Tussen-die-Riviere, Willem Pretorius; *Natal*: Giants Castle, Hluhluwe, Itala, Mkuzi, Ndumu, Oribi Gorge, Phinda, Royal Natal, Umfolozi; *Cape*: Andries Vosloo, Aughrabies, Bontebok, De Hoop, Gamkaberg, Gamkapoort, Hester Malan, Kalahari Gemsbok, Karoo, Keurboom, Kommandodrift, Mkambati, Mountain Zebra, Oviston, Rolfontein, Salmon's Dam, Tsitsikamma Coastal, Tsitsikamma Forest, Vaalbos, Zuurberg.

NAMIBIA: Daan Viljoen, Eastern & Western Caprivi, Etosha, Hardap Dam, Kaudom, Mahonga, Naukluft, Skeleton Coast, Von Bach, Waterberg Plateau; BOTSWANA: Chobe, Mashatu, Moremi; ZIMBABWE: Chete, Chewore, Chizarira, Gonarhezhou, Hwange, Malapati, Mana Pools, Matopos, Matusadona, Nyanga; MOZAMBIQUE: Gorongosa, Maputo Elephant.

✓ Vervet monkey

Cercopithecus pygerythrus

Blouaap

These are locally common and widely distributed in southern and central Africa. They are unmistakable and well-known. The Afrikaans name, blue monkey, is confusing in that the central African species, diademed guenon (*C. mitis*), which is closely related to the samango monkey and not the vervet, is also known as the blue monkey. The vervet, in turn, is very closely related to the green monkey (*C. aethiops*) of northern Africa.

They are diurnal, arboreal monkeys, which are equally at home on the ground. They are gregarious and form troops of up to 20 animals which peacefully aggregate into large groups at water holes or feeding grounds. The troop has a dominant male which maintains its status with grimacing and threatening gestures. Fights are usually one-sided, with the lower-scale animal redirecting its anger not at its attacker, but in turn to an animal of a lower status. Vocalisation is rather quiet in the wild state. The male utters a harsh 'kek-kek-kek' as a territory demarcation. They chirp and twitter in inter-troop communication, scream in alarm and terror.

Predominantly inhabitants of savanna woodlands they will penetrate deep into unsuitable habitat along treed water courses, and may even establish there if the vegetation is suitable, hence their presence along the riverine woodland of the Orange and Vaal rivers, although they are absent from the surrounding countryside.

Vervets sleep together in small groups, with similar status animals together. The troop is extremely protective of a juvenile. The male display of the blue scrotum and red penis on the front of the white belly is an important sexual manifestation and the male may also strut about with uplifted tail displaying its bright blue scrotum. The female in oestrus will display her swollen genitalia.

They are prey to most large predators, including leopard, caracal, serval, baboon, large raptors, particularly the crowned eagle and pythons. Usually one young, more rarely twins, is produced.

Food: Fruit, flowers, seed pods and leaves, as well as the gum of *Acacia* species, insects, caterpillars, spiders, lizards, bird's eggs and young birds. They are serious pests near to human habitation, where fearless pillaging of foodstuffs, even from inside the house, is common - also raid fruit and other crops causing considerable damage.

Common to very common

Distribution: SOUTH AFRICA: *Transvaal*: Ben Alberts, Borokalano, Doorndraai Dam, Hans Merensky, Hans Strydom Dam, Klaserie, Kruger Park, Langjan, Lapalala, Londolozi, Mala Mala, Manyeleti, Messina, Nyala Ranch, Nylsvley, Percy Fyfe, Pilanesberg, Rustenburg, Sabi-Sabi, Sabi-Sand, Timbavati, Umbabat/Motswari; *O.F.S.*: Soetdoring, Tussen-die-Riviere, Willem Pretorius; *Natal*: Hluhluwe, Mkuzi, Ndumu, Oribi Gorge, Phinda, St Lucia, Umfolozi; *Cape*: Addo Elephant, Amalinda, Andries Vosloo, Aughrabies, Doornkloof, Goukamma, Karoo, Keurboom, Kommandodrift, Mkambati, Mountain Zebra, Oviston, Rolfontein, Sandveld, Thomas Baines, Tsitsikamma Coastal, Tsitsikamma Forest, Vaalbos, Zuurberg.

NAMIBIA: Eastern & Western Caprivi, Etosha, Kaudom, Mahonga, Waterberg Plateau; BOTSWANA: Chobe, Makgadikgadi, Mashatu, Moremi; ZIMBABWE: Chete, Chewore, Chizarira, Gonarhezhou, Hwange, Matopos, Malapati, Mana Pools, Matusadona, Nyanga; MOZAMBIQUE: Gorongosa, Maputo Elephant.

Left fore

Left hind

³/₄ *actual size*

SAMANGO MONKEY	
Gestation period: ± 125 days	
Young: one, rarely twins	
Mass: ♂ 6 kg, ♀ 4,5 kg.	
Length: ♂ 135 cm, ♀ 115 cm.	
Life expectancy: unknown	

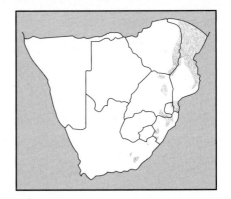

Samango monkey
Cercopithecus albogularis
Samango-aap

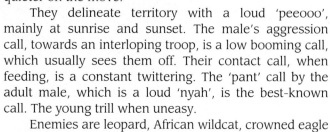

These monkeys are closely related to the blue monkey (*C. mitis*) and are known elsewhere as the white-throated guenon. They are much darker than the vervets and have dark brown faces. They are diurnal gregarious animals and live in troops of as many as 30 animals. In hot weather they are most active in the mornings and later afternoons, feeding in the higher tiers of the forest, descending lower and sometimes to the ground in the heat of the day to rest. They commonly associate with the vervets, but are quieter on the move.

They delineate territory with a loud 'peeooo', mainly at sunrise and sunset. The male's aggression call, towards an interloping troop, is a low booming call, which usually sees them off. Their contact call, when feeding, is a constant twittering. The 'pant' call by the adult male, which is a loud 'nyah', is the best-known call. The young trill when uneasy.

Enemies are leopard, African wildcat, crowned eagle and python. One young is produced and rarely twins.

Food: Ripe wild fruit, flowers, seeds, *Acacia karoo* gum, caterpillars, insects, young birds, bird's eggs. Also raid crops.

Distribution: SOUTH AFRICA: *Transvaal*: Kruger Park; *Natal*: Hluhluwe, Mkuzi, Ndumu, Phinda, Oribi Gorge, St Lucia; *Cape*: Mkambati.

Very rare and localised

ZIMBABWE: Chewore; MOZAMBIQUE: Gorongosa, Maputo Elephant.

Pangolin
Manis temminckii
Ietermagog or **Ietermagô**

These unmistakable animals are not related to the armadillos of south and central America, which they resemble superficially. They are nocturnal myrmacophagous (ant-eating) animals, which are heavily armoured with overlapping, imbricated, heavy scales. The edges of the scales of the tail are sharp and are formidable weapons, which the animals use in a sideways

Left fore

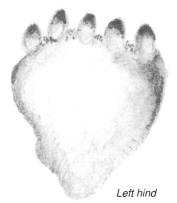

Left hind

Actual size

PANGOLIN
Gestation period: ± 145 days
Young: one
Mass: 16 kg.
Length: 80 cm.
Life expectancy: 12 years

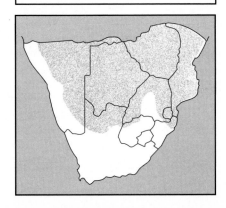

swipe. They also exude a waxy foul-smelling secretion from anal glands. Their ears have soft hair inside and the small eyes are set on soft, bulbous protuberances. The front claws are long, curved and sharp. They too are formidable weapons, but their primary function is digging and breaking open of the hard packed soil of ant's nests.

Widespread, seldom seen

They are solitary, relatively little-known animals, almost exclusively nocturnal, with some diurnal activity recorded. They live in appropriated burrows, although it is reported that they do sometimes dig their own. Only one rather precocial young is produced, which accompanies the mother for a long period. In stress they will be rolled into the mother's underparts. Pangolin are shy and will 'freeze' if danger is detected and are easily overlooked. They walk with the tail off the ground and when investigating the surroundings, will stand up on their hind legs, balancing on their broad tail and will sniff the wind. They are able to make off at some speed but, if touched or under extreme stress, they will curl up in a tight ball, with head inside, fully protecting their soft underparts. It is unwise to attempt to uncurl them as this is firstly almost impossible, and secondly, the tail will slide from side to side and may severely lacerate fingers.

They are generally immune to attack from anything as their habit of rolling into a ball prevents access to them and their foul-smelling urine, anal discharge and droppings repels any would-be predator. Man and the change of the environment is probably the one factor which will wipe out the pangolin. One young is produced.

Food: Their food is almost exclusively formacid ants also termites and the eggs, larvae and pupae. Their long glutinous tongues are inserted into the burrows of the nest, which have been broken open by the powerful claws, and then are withdrawn, covered with ants, eggs, larvae, pupae and much grit. Surface ants are licked up. Pangolins have no teeth and the food mass is ground up in the muscular sections of the stomach, with the grit probably aiding the process.

Distribution: SOUTH AFRICA: *Transvaal*: Ben Lavin, Borokalano, Hans Merensky, Hans Strydom Dam, Klaserie, Kruger Park, Langjan, Londolozi, Mala Mala, Manyeleti, Messina, Nyala Ranch, Pilanesberg, Sabi-Sabi, Sabi-Sand, Timbavati, Umbabat/Motswari; *Natal*: Hluhluwe, Mkuzi, Ndumu, Phinda, St Lucia; *Cape*: Kalahari Gemsbok, Vaalbos.

NAMIBIA: Daan Viljoen, Etosha, Hardap Dam, Kaudom, Mahonga, Von Bach, Waterberg Plateau; BOTSWANA: Chobe, Khutse, Mashatu, Moremi, Nxai Pan; ZIMBABWE: Chete, Chewore, Chizarira, Gonarhezhou, Hwange, Malapati, Mana Pools, Matopos, Matusadona, Nyanga; MOZAMBIQUE: Gorongosa, Maputo Elephant.

HARES & RABBITS

Three species are dealt with in detail in this guide, these are the Cape hare, the scrub hare and the riverine rabbit. Apart from the introduced rabbit, or European rabbit (*Oryctolagus cuniculus*), which is feral on Possession island, off Namibia; on Dassen, Jutten, Robben, Schaapen and Vondeling Islands, off the Cape south west coast; and on Bird and Seal islands, off the Cape south east coast, three other species are recorded in the sub-region. These are Smith's red rock rabbit (*Pronolagus rupestris*), the Natal red rock rabbit (*Pronolagus crassicaudatus*) and Jameson's red rock rabbit (*Pronolagus randensis*). Numbers of European rabbits have escaped captivity in the hinterland, but predator pressure does not seem to permit their continued survival.

All species of *Pronolagus* have similar habits and habitat requirements. Not unlike the dassie, they are found in rocky hills, valleys, boulder-covered kopjes and boulder piles in dry riverbeds from which they are unwilling to stray far. They are gregarious, but forage alone. Unlike the dassies, however, they are mainly nocturnal. Excepting for Jameson's red rock rabbit, which is very common in Zimbabwe's Matopos and the sandstone kopjes of the surrounding areas and into eastern Botswana, they are uncommon. Rabbit-like in appearance, they have shorter ears than *Lepus*.

The general distinction between rabbits and hares, apart from a different chromosomal count, is that rabbits are gregarious and hares solitary. The hind legs of hares are longer than the forelegs; this is marked in the rabbits. The physiological difference in the skulls allow the hares to breathe in far more air than the rabbits – necessary as they are considerably more mobile and active. Hares are precocial (able to look after themselves at birth) and rabbits are altricial (unable to look after themselves).

Controversy existed as to whether *Pronolagus* and *Bunolagus* should be regarded as hares or rabbits, but it seems, in view of the above differences evident in these two genera, that there is now consensus of opinion in that they should be regarded as rabbits.

✓ Cape Hare

Lepus capensis

Vlakhaas

The epithet *capensis* (from the Cape), allocated to this species by Linnaeus was an unfortunate choice as the animals are common in many parts of Africa, the Middle East and throughout Asia as far east as Mongolia. The Afrikaans name 'Vlakhaas' (hare of the open spaces) is far more suitable as they prefer open habitat. Smaller than the scrub hare, they are predomi-

³/₄ actual size

Left fore

Left hind

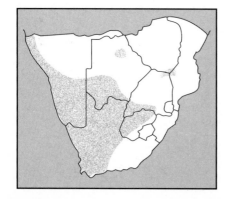

CAPE HARE

Gestation period: ± 42 days

Young: one – six, usually two – four

Mass: ♂ 1,5 kg, ♀ 2 kg.

Length: ♂ 55 cm, ♀ 58 cm.

Life expectancy: 10 – 12 years

nantly nocturnal but may venture out on overcast days although not in inclement and cold weather. In the day they lie up in 'forms' located in clumps of grass or under bushes. They lie quite still, flat on the ground, with hair and ears pressed closely to the body. If approached too closely they take off in a zig-zag course with ears erect. Under extreme stress they travel very fast with ears held flat and are able to change course very sharply to escape danger. They will, also, under extreme stress, seek refuge in another animal's burrow, a factor not observed in the scrub hare.

Very rare and localised

The habitat requirement of the Cape hare is markedly different to that of the scrub hare. They are able to tolerate very arid conditions and seem to stay with these drier conditions within their range. Where seen in wetter conditions they occur on the less vegetated fringes of woodland and grassland, such as at pans.

They are mostly mute but utter a shrill scream of fear. Males growl when courting or fighting; the young growl and squeak and jump like frogs if touched. Females call the young with a soft piping.

Enemies are many: all larger predators, including larger raptors and snakes. Crows, gulls and storks take the young. The adults defend their young from the smaller predators. In anger they stamp their forefeet and gnash their teeth. They use their formidable back legs with effect in a fight. One to six, usually two to four, young are produced.

Food: They are grazers, preferring areas with short grass.

Distribution: SOUTH AFRICA: *Transvaal*: Barberspan, Kruger Park, S A Lombard; *O.F.S.*: Bloemhof Dam, Erfenis Dam, Golden Gate, Hendrik Verwoerd Dam, Maria Maroka, Soetdoring, Tussen-die-Riviere, Willem Pretorius; *Cape*: Addo Elephant, Bontebok, Botsalano, De Hoop, Doornkloof, Gamkaberg, Gamkapoort, Hester Malan, Kalahari Gemsbok, Karoo, Kommandodrift, Langebaan, Mkambati, Mountain Zebra, Oviston, Rocher Pan, Rolfontein, Salmon's Dam, Sandveld, Vaalbos, Zuurberg.

NAMIBIA: Hardap Dam, Naukluft; BOTSWANA: Gemsbok, Mabuasehube, Makgadikgadi, Nxai Pan; ZIMBABWE: Hwange.

√ Scrub hare
Lepus saxatilis
Kolhaas

9

These hares are larger than the Cape hares and the size is variable over their range. They are generally largest in the south. Most animals have a

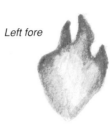

Left fore

Left hind

³/₄ actual size

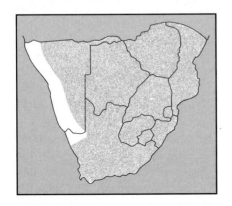

SCRUB HARE	
Gestation period: ± 35 days	
Young: one – three	
Mass: ♂ 2 kg, ♀ 2,6 kg.	
Length: ♂ 55 cm, ♀ 58 cm.	
Life expectancy: 8 years	

Widespread and common

distinct white spot on the forehead, from where the Afrikaans - 'kol' (spot) is derived. They are nocturnal, sensitive to weather conditions and are more in evidence in warmer than in cooler evenings. They lie up in forms under scrub, with ears and fur flattened, like the Cape hare and, if disturbed, run off rapidly with ears held flat, jinking irregularly.

Their habitat is mostly scrubby country and savannah woodland, where there is significant grassland. They are absent from desert and forests but common in agriculturally developed areas. They are usually silent but squeal loudly and kick savagely with the back legs and bite if handled.

Their enemies are similar to those of the Cape hares. One to three young are produced, usually two.

Food: They are predominantly grazers, living on the stems and rhizomes of grass. They prefer greener grass.

Distribution: Present in all reserves with the exception of Naukluft and Skeleton Coast in Namibia; Golden Gate in the O.F.S. and Hester Malan in the Cape.

Riverine rabbit
Bunolagus monticularis
Rivierkonyn

10

These very rare, little-known solitary rabbits, regarded as probably the rarest of South Africa's mammals, are also known as the 'Bushman hare'. They are similar to, but smaller than, the red rock rabbit. An early zoologist was reputed to have offered a pound to the local population for the capture of a riverine rabbit and, thereafter, it was widely known as the 'pondhaas'. They have unusually long ears and a diffused band of dark hair extending from under the mouth to below the ears, where it tails away upwards. The upper coat is grizzled and there is a patch of rich rufous hair on the nape of the neck. Unlike most other rabbits, the white scut or 'flag' (the underpart of the raised tail displayed when the animal runs off), is absent.

They are predominantly nocturnal and are most active at sunrise and sunset preferring the riparian scrub of the usually dry rivers in the arid areas of its range. Unlike the hares of the region, it is very slow-footed, runs along with its tail hanging down and is easily caught.

RIVERINE RABBIT
Gestation period: unknown
Young: one, rarely two
Mass: unknown
Length: 43 cm.
Life expectancy: unknown

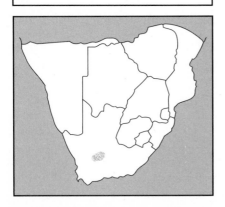

Spoor unknown

Their chief danger is from dogs, which however, are often unable to follow the rabbit into the thick shrubbery. Presumably they are prey also for black-backed jackals, caracal and other small predators, such as raptors. One, very occasionally two, altricial young are born in a breeding stop, which is dug in wind-formed hummocks under the roots of large shrubs.

Food: They are mainly browsers, and subsist on karoo bushes. Mesems are relished and grass is sometimes eaten.

Distribution: SOUTH AFRICA: *Cape*: Karoo National Park.

Porcupine
Hystrix africaeaustralis
Ystervark

11

Also known as the South African crested porcupine, these rodents are unmistakable. The erectile crest or mane consists of long white bristles along the central line of the neck. The quills are long, hard and sharp and are alternately banded in black and white. The bristles (or 'rattle-quills') at the end of the tail are thick, hollow, open at the end and more than 6 cm long. The spines, quills and crest are erected at will and, when erect, double the size of the animal and present a very sharp, formidable array of weaponry. When threatened or cornered, it reacts by stamping its feet, erecting its quills and rattling its tail bristles.

Porcupine act aggressively, turning their backs on a tormentor to charge swiftly backwards and anything not agile enough can be seriously injured by being deeply impaled on the hard, sharp detachable quills. If they are pursued they may stop suddenly and the pursuer is brought up short in a forest of sharp quills. Predators sometimes carry these quills around deeply embedded in their faces; these may cause sepsis and eventually kill the unfortunate animals.

Porcupine are nocturnal, active at dusk and through the night, sleeping by day in their burrows, but may sometimes sunbathe outside. They are usually solitary, but are seen in pairs or females with pre-weaned young. They prefer broken country with shelter places, which can be rocky crevices or caves. They take over disused antbear burrows, adapting them for their own use, but do not appear to excavate their own as the east African animals do.

Enemies are ground predators, up to the size of leopard and lion, but

PORCUPINE
Gestation period: ± 90 days
Young: one – four, usually two
Mass: ♂ 12 kg, ♀ 13 kg.
Length: ♂ 75 cm, ♀ 78 cm.
Life expectancy: up to 15 years, usually 8

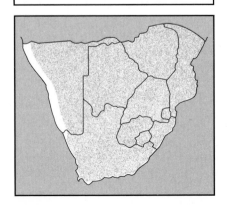

Right fore

²/₃ actual size

Right hind

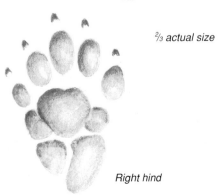

only if they are hungry enough to face the sharp spines. The safest form of attack used is to roll the porcupine over and get at the soft, unprotected underparts. One to four, usually two, young are produced in a grass lined hollow in the burrow.

Food: They are mainly vegetarian, but are recorded eating carrion. They will carry bones back to their burrows to gnaw at for the calcium content and are also recorded as gnawing at ivory tusks. Porcupine can become serious pests as they relish crops, particularly maize.

Widespread and common

Distribution: SOUTH AFRICA: *Transvaal*: Ben Alberts, Ben Lavin, Blyde River Canyon, Doorndraai Dam, Klaserie, Kruger Park, Langjan, Lapalala, Londolozi, Loskop Dam, Mala Mala, Manyeleti, Messina, Nyala Ranch, Nylsvley, Pilanesberg, Roodeplaat Dam, Rustenburg, Sabi-Sabi, Sabi-Sand, S A Lombard, Suikerbosrand, Timbavati, Umbabat/Motswari; *O.F.S.*: Bloemhof Dam, Erfenis Dam, Soetdoring, Tussen-die-Riviere, Willem Pretorius; *Natal*: Giants Castle, Hluhluwe, Mkuzi, Ndumu, Oribi Gorge, Phinda, Royal Natal, St Lucia, Umfolozi; *Cape*: Addo Elephant, Amalinda, Andries Vosloo, Aughrabies, Bontebok, De Hoop, Doornkloof, Gamkaberg, Gamkapoort, Goukamma, Hester Malan, Kalahari Gemsbok, Karoo, Keurboom, Kommandodrift, Langebaan, Mountain Zebra, Oviston, Robberg, Rocher Pan, Rolfontein, Salmon's Dam, Sandveld, Thomas Baines, Tsitsikamma Coastal, Tsitsikamma Forest, Vaalbos, Zuurberg.

NAMIBIA: Daan Viljoen, Eastern & Western Caprivi, Etosha, Hardap Dam, Kaudom, Mahonga, Naukluft, Skeleton Coast, Von Bach, Waterberg Plateau; BOTSWANA: Central Kalahari, Chobe, Gemsbok, Mabuasehube, Makgadikgadi, Mashatu, Moremi, Nxai Pan; ZIMBABWE: Chete, Chewore, Chizarira, Gonarhezhou, Hwange, Malapati, Mana Pools, Matopos, Matusadona, Nyanga; MOZAMBIQUE: Gorongosa, Maputo Elephant.

Springhaas
Pedetes capensis
Springhaas

12

Springhaas, also incorrectly known as springhares, have no known family relationship with any other animals and are not related to hares in any way. They are nocturnal animals, active from dusk to morning, but usually remain in the burrows in cold or wet weather. They inhabit sandy country, which is necessary for the construction of their burrows, preferring open country and generally avoiding areas of heavy grass cover.

Springhaas are large rodents, resembling small kangaroos. Their locomotion consists mainly of bounds and hops on powerful hind legs, with the tail thrown from side to side. Their colour varies but the black tip to their tails is always present. Whiskers are long and sensitive and, interspersed over the animal's bodies, there are long sensory hairs which, together with the whiskers, orientate the animals in their burrow systems. The ears and

SPRINGHAAS	
Gestation period: ± 70 days	
Young: one, rarely twins	
Mass: 3 kg.	
Length: 80 cm.	
Life expectancy: 7,5 years (in captivity)	

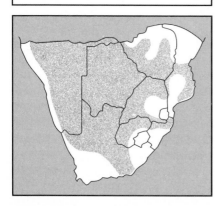

Left fore

Left hind

Actual size

nostrils are closed by folds of skin during burrowing activity. The front curved claws are adapted to breaking ground and the powerful rear feet throw the soil out well clear of the burrow. The strong incisor teeth cut effortlessly through roots.

When caught in a beam of light they squat and lower their head but shortly rise up with ears raised, inquisitively examining the source of the disturbance. Because of the shape of their heads only one eye, as a point of light bobbing up and down, is seen in a beam of light and this feature distinguishes it from other nocturnal animals. The voice is a grunting as a contact call, a soft piping if afraid, and a loud bleat if in great danger. They are, however, usually silent.

The springhaas has many predators - honey badgers, mongooses, striped weasels, caracals, servals, African wildcats, genets, pythons, jackals, large owls and monitor lizards. One of the main predators is indigenous man, who takes large quantities of the springhaas for food.

One young, rarely two, is produced, which is ready to sit on its hind legs almost immediately after birth and is active and able to run about after two days, when its eyes open.

Uncommon and
localised

Food: Particularly the rhizomes of grass, grass, herbs, cultivated crops and also insects.

Distribution: SOUTH AFRICA: *Transvaal*: Barberspan, Ben Lavin, Blyde River Canyon, Borokalano, Doorndraai Dam, Kruger Park, Langjan, Lapalala, Manyeleti, Messina, Nyala Ranch, Nylsvley, Percy Fyfe, Roodeplaat Dam, Sabi-Sabi, Sabi-Sand, S A Lombard, Sterkspruit, Suikerbosrand, Umbabat/Motswari; *O.F.S.*: Bloemhof Dam, Erfenis Dam, Golden Gate, Hendrik Verwoerd Dam, Tussen-die-Riviere; *Natal*: False Bay, Hluhluwe, Itala, Mkuzi, Ndumu, Phinda, Umfolozi, Weenen; *Cape*: Addo Elephant, Amalinda, Andries Vosloo, Aughrabies, Botsalano, Doornkloof, Hester Malan, Kalahari Gemsbok, Keurboom, Kommandodrift, Mountain Zebra, Oviston, Rolfontein, Sandveld, Vaalbos; SWAZILAND: Pongola.

NAMIBIA: Daan Viljoen, Eastern & Western Caprivi, Etosha, Hardap Dam, Kaudom, Mahonga; BOTSWANA: Chobe, Gemsbok, Khutse, Mabuasehube, Makgadikgadi, Mashatu, Moremi, Nxai Pan; ZIMBABWE: Gonarhezhou, Hwange, Matopos; MOZAMBIQUE: Maputo Elephant.

SQUIRRELS

Six endemic squirrels are found in the subregion and one introduced feral animal. The grey squirrel *Sciurus carolinensis*, was introduced by Cecil John Rhodes, from the United States of America to the gardens of Grootte Schuur in c.1900. They have proliferated until they are a common sight in and around Cape Town and their range now extends as far as Ceres and Worcester in the east, Grabouw in the south and perhaps Malmesbury in the north. Only two of the six endemics are dealt with in this account. The others are summarised as follows:

The mountain ground squirrel (*Xerus princeps*) which is a rare, rock-dwelling animal, differs from *X. inauris* by having three black bands on the tail hairs instead of two, proportionately larger eye orbits, and yellow, instead of white, incisors. They occur from Beerseba in southern Namibia, following the ridge of the escarpment to Kaokoveld and into Angola.

The sun squirrel (*Heliosciurus rufobrachium*) occurs in eastern Zimbabwe and northern and southern Mozambique. They are the largest of the arboreal squirrels and the tail is much more clearly banded than any other squirrel in the subregion.

The striped tree squirrel (*Funisciurus congicus*) is a west central African endemic with its range extending narrowly into north western Namibia. It is a woodland species which differs from its near relative, *Paraxerus cepapi*, in being the smallest squirrel in the subregion, in having shorter tail hair, and longitudinal white body stripes.

The range of the red squirrel (*Paraxerus palliatus*) is eastern Mozambique and narrowly into northern Zululand as far south as Ngoye Forest. They differ from other squirrels in the subregion in being redder in colour and having yellower or redder coloured tails. The habitat requirement is moist evergreen forests and woodland, in contrast to its closest relative *P. cepapi*, which requires more open savanna habitat.

√ Ground squirrel

Xerus inauris

Waaierstertgrondeekhoring

13

These lovable squirrels are characteristic inhabitants of the more arid western/central parts of the subregion, where they are endemic. They prefer habitat which has a hard substrate as loose sandy soil makes burrow construction difficult. They are frequent on the edges of dry pans, which are plentiful in their range. The characteristic white longitudinal body stripe is a diagnostic feature, except that it is also present in the much rarer *X. princeps* and *Heliosciurus rufobrachium*. These two animals and their characteristics have been discussed previously.

Ground squirrels are diurnal, gregarious animals living in colonies of as many as 30 animals. The warrens are a series of complicated tunnels with many openings and dead-ends, often shared with yellow mongooses and suricates. They are self-dug by these avid diggers and roots are sheared through with their sharp incisors. Fresh burrows are characterised

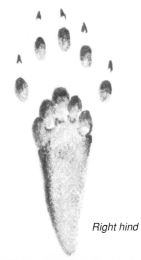

Right fore

Actual size

Right hind

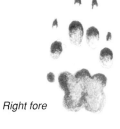

GROUND SQUIRREL
Gestation period: ± probably 45 days
Young: one – three
Mass: ♂ 650 g, ♀ 600 g.
Length: 46 cm.
Life expectancy: 7 years

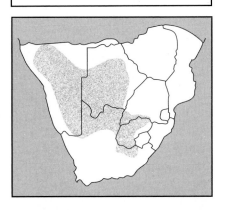

by the crater-shaped mounds of fresh soil at the entrances. The groups consist of females and young, with the males moving between groups, only being accepted when females are in oestrus. They will then be accepted temporarily as a member of the group.

The dominant female defends the burrow from any squirrel from other groups, chasing them away even back to their own burrows. Other females also defend the burrows, but with less enthusiasm. Play between juveniles and sub-adults is frequent.

When danger is perceived they may wave their tails up and down and give voice to a high-pitched whistling alarm rising to a scream in serious danger. They growl during play and aggression and the young utter a 'chip-chip'. They are sensitive to the warning voice of the blacksmith and crowned plovers.

They are prey to larger mongooses, African wild cats, small-spotted cats, caracals, Cape fox, jackals, large raptors and snakes. One to three young are produced.

Food: They are mainly vegetarian living on karoid bushes, succulent plants, curcubits, bulbs and grass, but will eat some insect food.

Distribution: SOUTH AFRICA: *Transvaal*: Barberspan, Blyde River Canyon, S A Lombard; *O.F.S.*: Bloemhof Dam, Erfenis Dam, Hendrik Verwoerd Dam, Maria Maroka, Soetdoring, Tussen-die-Riviere, Willem Pretorius; *Cape*: Aughrabies, Botsalano, Doornkloof, Kalahari Gemsbok, Mountain Zebra, Oviston, Rolfontein, Sandveld, Vaalbos.

NAMIBIA: Daan Viljoen, Etosha, Hardap Dam, Naukluft, Von Bach, Waterberg Plateau; BOTSWANA: Central Kalahari, Gemsbok, Khutse, Mabuasehube, Makgadikgadi.

Tree squirrel

Paraxerus cepapi

Boomeekhoring

| 14 |

These all-brown diurnal squirrels, with lighter underparts, are a common feature of the drier savannah bushveld and woodland. Their undulating run along the ground and rapid passage up into a tree are both a common sight. These small animals are usually solitary but pairs, or a small party of a female and two young, may be seen. However, groups of two adult males or females, accompanied by sub-adults, or in the breeding season as many as seven young, live together. They will mob a predator, vocalising a penetrating clicking sound and flicking their tails, while sitting on a safe vantage point. Should the danger increase so will the intensity of the clicking, which will rise to a harsh rattle, while the tail-flicking tempo is similarly

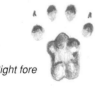

Right fore

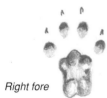

Right hind

Actual size

TREE SQUIRREL
Gestation period: ± 55 days
Young: one – three
Mass: ♂ 190 g, ♀ 195 g.
Length: 35 cm.
Life expectancy: 8 years

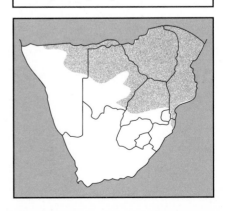

increased. In extreme danger they will utter a high-pitched whistle.

A common sight in the bushveld is an individual about to enter a nesting hole and being confronted by the occupant. Nose to nose mutual sniffing will ensue and, if the visitor is from the same group, it will be allowed to visit, but if not, will be chased off. They are very agile in their arboreal habitat, able to leap for distances up to 2 metres. They forage on the ground and when disturbed tend to head for their nesting hole, which may mean leaping from tree to tree. They also habitually lie flat on a branch, relying on camouflage and waiting for the danger to pass. They also tend to place themselves behind a branch or tree trunk away from perceived danger.

Abundant and widespread

Their nests are in holes in trees, generally made by woodpeckers; these are grass and leaf-lined. Their vocalisation, apart from the alarms, is a long drawn-out 'tchuk-tchuk-tchuk' interspersed with single 'tchuks', which are accompanied by tail-flicking.

Enemies are mongooses, caracal, genets, larger birds of prey and pythons. One to three, usually two, young are produced.

Food: They are predominantly vegetarians, eating the flowers, leaves, bark, fruit and tender shoots of a wide variety of trees. Both sexes bury hard food, such as nuts, in scattered localities. They are very secretive about doing this and never do so in the presence of another squirrel. Despite this stealing does take place.

Distribution: SOUTH AFRICA: *Transvaal*: Barberspan, Ben Alberts, Ben Lavin, Blyde River Canyon, Borokalano, Doorndraai Dam, Hans Merensky, Hans Strydom Dam, Klaserie, Kruger Park, Langjan, Lapalala, Londolozi, Mala Mala, Manyeleti, Messina, Nyala Ranch, Nylsvley, Ohrigstad Dam, Percy Fyfe, Pilanesberg, Rustenburg, Sabi-Sabi, Sabi-Sand, Sterkspruit, Timbavati, Umbabat/Motswari.

NAMIBIA: Eastern & Western Caprivi, Kaudom, Mahonga, Waterberg Plateau; BOTSWANA: Chobe, Makgadikgadi, Mashatu, Moremi; ZIMBABWE: Chete, Chewore, Chizarira, Gonarhezhou, Hwange, Malapati, Matopos, Matusadona, Nyanga; MOZAMBIQUE: Gorongosa, Maputo Elephant.

AARDWOLF & HYAENAS

There is one aardwolf and three hyaena types in Africa. The striped hyaena (*Crocuta hyaena*) is found only in the northern hemisphere. The aardwolf is the only extant representative of its subfamily *Protelinae*. The only two hyaenas of this sub-region are the spotted and the brown hyaenas. Both animals have the typical hyaena build - higher at the shoulders than at the rump, massive head and shoulders and broad powerful jaws with the extra weight carried on the forefeet. These are larger than the rear feet, which fact is clearly revealed in the spoor.

The obvious features which distinguish the one hyaena from the other are: the spotted coat and rounded ears of the spotted hyaena and the unspotted ears and pointed ears of the brown hyaena. The female spotted hyaena is heavier than the male and the male brown hyaena is heavier than the female. Despite their dog-like appearance, these members of this Hyaenidae family are more closely related to the Felidae, the cat family. The closest relationship is, however, with the mongooses, of the family Viverridae.

Aardwolf

Proteles cristatus

Aardwolf

15

The aardwolf is a nocturnal, dog-like, myrmacophagous (ant-eating) animal, differing from other ant-eaters, such as the pangolin and antbear, in having no elongated snout, but having a long thin tongue and powerful digging claws. They have four digits on the hind paws and five on the forepaws and are equipped with strong canines which they use for defence and not to kill stock, as is commonly and erroneously believed. In fact the peg-like molars are unsuited to a carnivorous diet. They avoid using their canines in defence, relying rather on their formidable appearance. Because of an ignorant belief in their involvement in stock destruction, they are relentlessly persecuted and are often innocent victims of packs of dogs set in pursuit of black-backed jackals. Generally solitary, will sometimes pair or form family parties.

When stressed they raise the erectile crest along their spine and appear twice their real size. This is accompanied by a deep-throated growling, ending in an explosive bark. When severely threatened their roaring is surprisingly loud for so small an animal. If forced they will defend themselves bravely from dogs and other attackers.

The preferred habitat is open grassy plains. They use disused holes of antbears or springhaas as a lair. They are vigorous diggers, shaping these holes to suit their needs and are also believed to dig their own burrows.

Their enemies, apart from man and his dog, are leopards, lion, spotted hyaena and pythons. Two to four, usually three, altricial blind young are born in the burrow and are fed on regurgitated termites.

Food: Very specialised feeders, eating only termites. The main food in the

AARDWOLF
Gestation period: ± 90 days
Young: two – four, usually three
Mass: ♂ 9 kg, ♀ 8 kg.
Length: ♂ 90 cm, ♀ 95 cm.
Life expectancy: 10 – 12 years

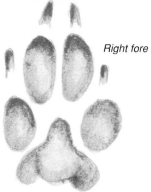

Right fore

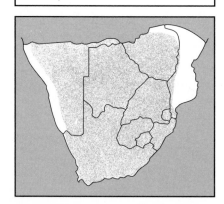

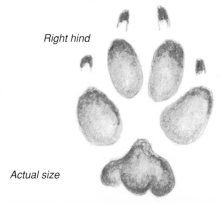

Right hind

Actual size

sub-region are the nasute, poorly-pigmented, nocturnal *Trinervitermes trinervoides* termites, which emerge up to twenty metres from their mound in dense foraging parties. These are located by smell and hearing and are simply licked off the ground by the long, glutinous, mobile tongue, as many as 300 000 termites a night. In the winter, when it is often too cold for *T.trinervoides* to emerge, the aardwolf will then be obliged to forage diurnally on the true harvester termites (*Hodotermes mossambicus*), which are well pigmented and, being able to stand the sun, are diurnal and are also particularly active in winter. They are not dependent on water being available.

Rare and localised

The aardwolf is as successful as it is because the other ant-eaters, unlike the aardwolf, will not eat the *trinervitermes* because of its chemical defense, a very sticky, noxious, terpene-based liquor, which is produced in a frontal gland (hence 'nasute termite') and squirted out of the frontal squirt of the soldiers.

Distribution: SOUTH AFRICA: *Transvaal*: Ben Lavin, Borokalano, Doorndraai Dam, Hans Merensky, Kruger Park, Lapalala, Manyeleti, Messina, Nyala Ranch, Nylsvley, Pilanesberg, Roodeplaat Dam, Rustenburg, Sabi-Sabi, Sabi-Sand, S A Lombard, Suikerbosrand, Timbavati, Umbabat/Motswari; *O.F.S.*: Erfenis Dam, Golden Gate, Maria Maroka, Soetdoring, Tussen-die-Riviere, Willem Pretorius; *Natal*: Giants Castle, Hluhluwe, Mkuzi, Ndumu, Phinda, St Lucia, Umfolozi; *Cape*: Addo Elephant, Andries Vosloo, Aughrabies, Bontebok, Botsalano, Doornkloof, Gamkaberg, Gamkapoort, Hester Malan, Kalahari Gemsbok, Karoo, Kommandodrift, Mountain Zebra, Oviston, Rolfontein, Sandveld, Vaalbos, Zuurberg.

NAMIBIA: Daan Viljoen, Eastern & Western Caprivi, Etosha, Hardap Dam, Kaudom, Mahonga, Naukluft, Skeleton Coast, Von Bach, Waterberg Plateau; BOTSWANA: Central Kalahari, Chobe, Gemsbok, Khutse, Mabuasehube, Makgadikgadi, Mashatu, Moremi, Nxai Pan; ZIMBABWE: Chete, Chewore, Chizarira, Gonarhezhou, Hwange, Mana Pools, Matopos.

Spotted hyaena

Crocuta crocuta

Gevlekte hiëna

16

Spotted hyaenas are creatures of the open woodland, open savannah, and semi desert. They are predominantly scavengers but are also active and relentless hunters. Their existence depends upon a large supply of game and their disappearance in certain parts reflects the impact of man upon their environment. They are active mainly at dusk and night and occasionally by day. They sleep in self-dug or appropriated burrows, in tall grass or rock piles. They roll in mud, carrion or regurgitated food and indulge in mutual licking and grooming.

SPOTTED HYAENA

Gestation period: ± 110 days

Young: one – four, usually two

Mass: ♂ 60 kg, ♀ 70 kg.

Shoulder height: ♂ 85 cm, ♀ 86 cm.

Length: ♂ 155 cm, ♀ 160 cm.

Life expectancy: up to 40 years in captivity

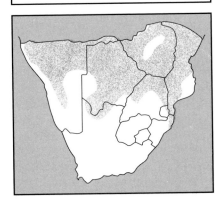

Right fore

Right hind

¹/₃ *actual size*

Their voice is an integral 'sound of an African night', a succession of long drawn-out whoops, beginning low on the scale and rising in cadence and up the scale, ending in a low moaning, at the gathering together for the hunt. Their other vocalisations are hysterical giggling after a successful hunt, yelling when attempting to drive off an enemy, whining, grunting and groaning.

The spotted hyaena family is a matriarchal society, in which the heavier female is the undisputed ruler of the clan. There is usually a single dominant male, which defers to the ruling matriarch. The females have external genitalia, remarkably similar to those of the males, giving rise to an age-old myth that the spotted hyaenas are hermaphrodites.

Their main enemies are lion. Unguarded young and solitary animals fall prey to lions as well as to leopards and hunting dogs. The young are also vulnerable to old hyaena males and to other packs of spotted hyaena. The mutual savage hatred of the lion by the spotted hyaena is evidence of the long and bitter rivalry between the two species and the unrelenting harassment by each other at the kill. One to four, usually two, altricial pups are born.

Food: Predominantly carrion; their main food is from lion kills, capable even of consuming the thigh bone of a buffalo. As their senses are keen, they are generally the first to detect a carcass or a kill. They hunt old, sick and young herbivores and in some areas adult antelope and zebra are brought down by a bite to their fetlocks and then torn to pieces while still alive. While in a pack they may drive lions and other predators from their kills. Solitary humans may be at risk from the packs at night. Domestic stock is also taken with the break-in to stockades at night. Sheep, donkeys, horses and goats are taken and any loose offal or anything remotely edible is consumed. Other food is any small animals, crabs, also relishing the faeces of wild dogs. They eat grass and other vegetable matter and the contents of refuse bins at rest camps. The young also eat the faeces of ungulates. Very dependent on available water for which they will travel far.

Common to abundant and widespread

Distribution: SOUTH AFRICA: *Transvaal*: Hans Merensky, Klaserie, Kruger Park, Londolozi, Mala Mala, Manyeleti, Sabi-Sabi, Sabi-Sand, Timbavati, Umbabat/Motswari; *Natal*: Hluhluwe, Mkuzi, Ndumu, Phinda, Umfolozi; *Cape*: Kalahari Gemsbok.

NAMIBIA: Eastern & Western Caprivi, Etosha, Kaudom, Mahonga, Naukluft, Skeleton Coast, Waterberg Plateau; BOTSWANA: Chobe, Gemsbok, Makgadikgadi, Mashatu, Moremi, Nxai Pan; ZIMBABWE: Chete, Chewore, Chizarira, Gonarhezhou, Hwange, Malapati, Mana Pools, Matopos, Matusadona; MOZAMBIQUE: Gorongosa.

Brown hyaena
Hyaena brunnea
Strandjut

Brown hyaenas are smaller and less aggressive than the spotted hyaena. As if to compensate they have a mane of erectile hair which, under stress, will stand up, increasing their apparent size and ferocious appearance. Their preferred habitat is desert, semi-desert, dry savannah, open scrub and open woodland. They favour rocky hills with bush cover.

The occurrence of brown hyaena is far less affected by their proximity to humans than is the occurrence of spotted hyaena. They have been found even within the larger cities within their range. They are predominantly nocturnal and crepuscular, very rarely diurnal. They seek out good shelter during the day, choosing such trees as the shepherd's bush (*Boscia albitrunca*) with a heavy branch cover near to the ground, or rocky crevices and deserted burrows and in winter thick bush suffices. They are solitary animals but will gather at large carcasses.

Their vocalisation is a loud owlish 'wah-wah-wah' at dusk, often repeated. They yowl, growl or whine while squabbling over food. Unlike the spotted hyaena they do not 'laugh' or giggle. Their senses are very well developed and they can detect food from a long distance.

Enemies are lions and spotted hyaena in packs. The young are also vulnerable to jackals, servals and caracals. Give birth to one to three, usually two, young in a burrow with a narrow entrance to exclude jackals and other predators while the parents are absent.

Food: The main fare is carrion from the kills of other predators, small prey of any kind (rodents, birds, eggs, reptiles and insects), fruit, poultry, and on the sea shore, any flotsam that is edible. They are not dependent upon available water.

Very rare and localised

Distribution: SOUTH AFRICA: *Transvaal*: Ben Lavin, Borokalano, Doorndraai Dam, Hans Merensky, Hans Strydom Dam, Kruger Park, Lapalala, Messina, Nyala Ranch, Nylsvley, Ohrigstad Dam, Pilanesberg, Rustenburg, Suikerbosrand; *Natal*: Hluhluwe, St Lucia, Umfolozi; *Cape*: Botsalano, Doornkloof, Kalahari Gemsbok, Rolfontein, Vaalbos.

NAMIBIA: Daan Viljoen, Etosha, Hardap Dam, Kaudom, Mahonga, Naukluft, Skeleton Coast, Waterberg Plateau; BOTSWANA: Central Kalahari, Gemsbok, Khutse, Mabuasehube, Makgadikgadi, Mashatu, Nxai Pan; ZIMBABWE: Gonarhezhou, Hwange, Matopos.

Left fore

Left hind

¹/₂ actual size

BROWN HYAENA
Gestation period: ± 90 days
Young: one – two (usually two, rarely three)
Mass: ♂ 40 kg, ♀ 30 kg.
Shoulder height: 79 cm.
Length: ♂ 145 cm, ♀ 140 cm.
Life expectancy: up to 24 years

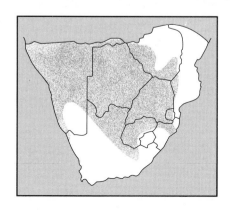

LION	
Gestation period: ± 110 days	
Young: one – six, usually two – three	
Mass: ♂ 230 kg, ♀ 160 kg.	
Length: ♂ 260 cm.	
Life expectancy: normally 15 years, 30 years in captivity	

Left fore

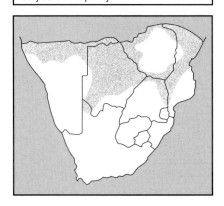

Left hind

¹/₃ actual size

LARGE CATS
Three large cats are endemic to the continent and all three occur in this sub-region.

✓
Lion
Panthera leo

Leeu

18

Lions are the largest of the African predators, the males can weigh up to 230 kg. The females are smaller and lighter. Only the male is maned and in very rare cases unmaned males have been recorded. The hair of the mane can be up to 18-20 cm in length and is usually brown, but black-maned animals are also encountered as are extremely rare cases of melanistic (black) lions, which have not been recorded from our sub-region. Rare, very light animals, commonly known as the 'White Lions of Timbavati', occur here.

These, the most sociable of the cats, form prides of 3 to 30 or more individuals, consisting of 1 dominant male 1 dominant female, several adult males and females, sundry sub-adults and cubs.

Lionesses form the nucleus of the pride, which is rarely moved beyond its established range. When the other young males in the pride are perceived by the dominant male to be a possible threat, it drives them away, when they

Lioness in the Kalahari

either join other prides if permitted, or if old and strong enough, form their own pride. The dominant male frequently has two prides and also ranges far and wide. Cubs and very young lions are in constant danger within the pride from irritable adults, particularly the dominant male, that will, with or without apparent provocation, sometimes lash out and maim or kill them.

Lions have a wide habitat tolerance, from desert conditions to fairly dense bush. They are absent from densely afforested areas. Because of their nomadic nature they are particularly vulnerable outside of conservation areas. Where there are unfenced reserves they will move beyond these safe havens after stock. This brings them into conflict with man and usually these errant lions will eventually be eliminated.

Lions are active at night, mainly around sunrise and early evening. In the day they laze away the hours in the shade, or move sluggishly around. The nocturnal hunting is a combined effort to frighten and confuse the prey. The male gives a mighty roar, which is heard across great distances, but the female usually does the killing. In the case of small prey, a swipe from a powerful paw is sufficient to kill it. Larger prey are killed by having their necks twisted and broken by a powerful wrench between the lion's forelegs and its jaws, which are clamped to the victim's neck. Larger animals are also suffocated by a powerful grip across the larynx or the muzzle.

One to six, usually three to four, altricial cubs are produced. When the pregnant female is ready to give birth, she leaves the pride, to rejoin only when the cubs are 4-8 weeks old, returning only if the older cubs already in the pride have weaned and will not be a danger through competition for food to the new arrivals. The birth rate among lions is fairly high, but so is the mortality rate. Loss is due to predation by such animals as hyaena, lack of sufficient food,or death by misadventure in the paws of the other members of the pride.

Common to uncommon and widespread

Food: An extremely wide range of food is consumed. Virtually anything palatable that moves, even insects, mice and up the size scale to buffalo or even elephant - if the lions are lucky. It would seem, however, that the wildebeest is the prime choice.

Distribution: SOUTH AFRICA: *Transvaal*: Klaserie, Kruger Park, Londolozi, Mala Mala, Manyeleti, Sabi-Sabi, Sabi-Sand, Timbavati, Umbabat/Motswari; *O.F.S.*: Soetdoring; *Natal*: Hluhluwe, Phinda, Umfolozi; *Cape*: Kalahari Gemsbok.

NAMIBIA: Eastern & Western Caprivi, Etosha, Kaudom, Mahonga, Skeleton Coast; BOTSWANA: Central Kalahari, Chobe, Gemsbok, Khutse, Mabuasehube, Makgadikgadi, Mashatu, Moremi, Nxai Pan; ZIMBABWE: Chete, Chewore, Chizarira, Gonarhezhou, Hwange, Malapati, Mana Pools, Matusadona, Nyanga; MOZAMBIQUE: Gorongosa.

Leopard
Panthera pardus
Luiperd

These solitary cats are the largest of the spotted cats of Africa. The weight of an adult male is about 60 kg and the female about 30 kg. The leopards of the mountains of the southern and south western Cape tend to be smaller. There is considerable colour variation over their range from India to southern Africa. The so-called 'black leopard' is more common in India, Somalia, Ethiopia and Zaïre and has also been encountered in South Africa.

Leopards are silent, secretive animals, whose vocalisation is a hoarse, rasping cough repeated at intervals. They move in a casual loping stride, or they may make off at a bouncing gallop, changing to a fast trot. All of their senses are well-developed as their efficient hunting reveals. They like to lie out on high vantage points in the mornings or late evenings, where they may watch for prey. They have a wide habitat tolerance, but prefer forests and the more hilly areas with rocky prominences and hiding places, bushy areas and tall grass with associated rocky places. They are also found in arid areas, where they will hide up in deserted antbear holes. True desert areas are unsuitable, but they may penetrate these areas along treed water-courses.

They are sometimes killed by lion, hunting dogs, spotted hyaenas and crocodiles. The young by hyaenas and jackals. Litters of one to six, usually three to four, altricial cubs are produced in caves or other sheltered places with plenty of cover. After about four months they will begin to accompany their mother and make their first kill at about five months.

Food: An extremely wide range of animal food is utilised. They are notorious man-eaters in certain parts of the world, but this is very rare in this sub-region. The major prey taken seems to be small and medium sized antelope, but this does not exclude the occasional larger antelope, such as the adult kudu, wildebeest and hartebeest. Baboons are a favoured fare, although leopards have serious trouble with the baboon troops if they foolishly attack a member of the clan too openly. Such animals as bushpigs and warthogs are taken as are jackals. Their liking for the domestic dog is notorious and places, such as the town of Kariba in Zimbabwe, have a distinct absence of these domestic pets. Unusual fare is snakes, porcupines,

Uncommon but more common in suitable habitat

LEOPARD
Gestation period: ± 100 days
Young: one – six, usually two – three
Mass: ♂ 60 kg, ♀ 30 kg.
Length: ♂ 200 cm, ♀ 180 cm.
Life expectancy: 21 years

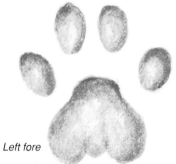

Left fore

Left hind

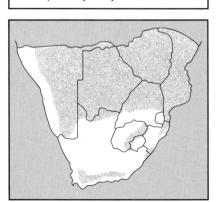

$^1/_2$ *actual size*

fish, domestic stock, birds such as guinea fowl, rats, mice and also carrion.

The strength of the leopard is clearly shown in their habit of dragging a very heavy kill up into high branches of a tree to protect it from other scavengers.

Distribution: SOUTH AFRICA: *Transvaal*: Ben Alberts, Ben Lavin, Borokalano, Doorndraai Dam, Hans Merensky, Hans Strydom Dam, Klaserie, Kruger Park, Langjan, Lapalala, Londolozi, Mala Mala, Manyeleti, Messina, Nyala Ranch, Nylsvley, Percy Fyfe, Pilanesberg, Rustenburg, Sabi-Sabi, Sabi-Sand, Suikerbosrand, Timbavati, Umbabat/Motswari; *Natal*: Giants Castle, Hluhluwe, Itala, Mkuzi, Ndumu, Oribi Gorge, Phinda, Royal Natal, St Lucia, Umfolozi; *Cape*: Aughrabies, Gamkaberg, Gamkapoort, Kalahari Gemsbok, Keurboom, Mountain Zebra, Robberg, Tsitsikamma Coastal, Tsitsikamma Forest, Zuurberg.

NAMIBIA: Daan Viljoen, Eastern & Western Caprivi, Etosha, Hardap Dam, Kaudom, Mahonga, Naukluft, Skeleton Coast, Von Bach, Waterberg Plateau; BOTSWANA: Central Kalahari, Chobe, Gemsbok, Khutse, Mabuasehube, Makgadikgadi, Mashatu, Moremi, Nxai Pan; ZIMBABWE: Chete, Chewore, Chizarira, Gonarhezhou, Hwange, Malapati, Mana Pools, Matopos, Matusadona, Nyanga; MOZAMBIQUE: Gorongosa, Maputo Elephant.

Cheetah

Acinonyx jubatus

Jagluiperd

20

The streamlined and elegant cheetah, although purported to attain speeds of over 100 km per hour, this only occurs for short bursts during the hunt, but it is, nevertheless, the fleetest animal on earth. Their claws, unlike the other cats of the region, are not able to be retracted. They are terrestrial animals, utilising stout sloping tree trunks to rest on and to use as observation posts. Predominantly diurnal they are most active in early morning and late afternoon. In hot weather they rest in the heat of the day, preferring an elevated position from where they can keep an eye out for danger. They are more solitary than social animals. Males form strongly cohesive bachelor groups. The females are not joined by the males except during oestrus.

Vocalisation is a curious chirruping, rather like a birdcall. This may be accompanied by a 'chirr' sound. When content they purr loudly and growl, cough, hiss or snarl. They raise the hair on their back when they threaten.

Cheetahs are not aggressive towards each other except where males battle over a female in oestrus. These can be serious skirmishes which may leave one of the contestants dead. Their habitat preferences are open plains, savanna woodland and semi-desert.

Their bad record of difficult breeding has been ascribed variously to an inbred genetic difficulty and, by some zoologists, to the possible occurrence of a serious plague in times past which wiped out most of the cheetah leaving very few survivors and insufficient unrelated individuals to

CHEETAH	
Gestation period: ± 93 days	
Young: one – six, usually two – four	
Mass: ♂ 50 kg, ♀ 40 kg.	
Length: ♂ 200 cm, ♀ 190 cm.	
Life expectancy: 16 years	

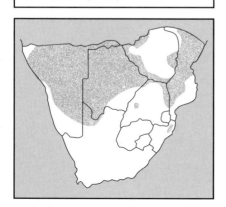

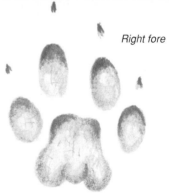

Right fore

½ actual size

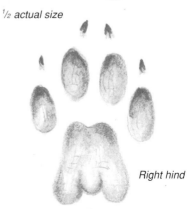

Right hind

King Cheetah

perpetuate a very viable gene pool. This would have inhibited successful ongoing breeding. They also have a complicated courtship process, which further increases the breeding problem.

The beautiful king cheetah is a genetically abberant animal which occasionally manifests in populations of cheetah in central and southern Zimbabwe, eastern Botswana, north eastern, northern and western Transvaal.

Lion and leopard are predators of the cheetah and lion and hyaenas chase the cheetah from its prey. A litter of one to six, usually two to four, altricial cubs are born in a rocky crevice. They are carefully hidden by the mother while she hunts. Despite this they often fall prey to predators.

Food: The principal food is made up by medium to small antelope or the young of the larger antelope. Cheetahs also prey on terrestrial birds up to the size of the ostrich. Hares, porcupines, springhaas, young warthogs and porcupines are also taken. When hunting is done in a pack they will sometimes separate a giraffe calf and pull it down. They are frequently injured when they tackle large

Fairly common in certain areas

CARACAL
Gestation period: ± 70 days
Young: one – six, usually two – three
Mass: ♂ 13 kg, ♀ 10 kg.
Length: ♂ 110 cm, ♀ 106 cm.
Life expectancy: 17 years

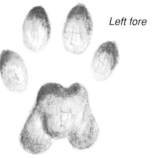

Left fore

½ actual size

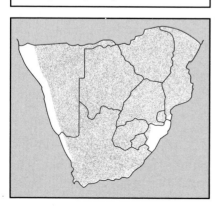

Left hind

prey such as buffalo, giraffe, wildebeest or zebra. They will avoid confrontation with a large herd of any animal, preferring to hunt the fringes, taking stragglers and young.

Before the hunt they survey the veld from a vantage point. After selection the prey is stalked up to about 70 metres. They then dash after the prey, relying upon their superior speed. If this dash is unsuccessful they abandon that particular animal and start again.

Distribution: SOUTH AFRICA: *Transvaal*: Klaserie, Kruger Park, Londolozi, Mala Mala, Manyeleti, Pilanesberg, Sabi-Sabi, Sabi-Sand, Suikerbosrand, Timbavati, Umbabat/Motswari; *Natal*: Hluhluwe, Mkuzi, Phinda, St Lucia, Umfolozi; *Cape*: Kalahari Gemsbok, Rolfontein.

NAMIBIA: Daan Viljoen, Etosha, Hardap Dam, Kaudom, Mahonga, Naukluft, Skeleton Coast, Von Bach, Waterberg Plateau; BOTSWANA: Central Kalahari, Chobe, Gemsbok, Khutse, Mabuasehube, Mashatu, Moremi, Nxai Pan; ZIMBABWE: Chewore, Chizarira, Gonarhezhou, Hwange, Mana Pools, Matopos.

SMALL CATS

There are six small cat species endemic to Africa of which four occur in this sub-region. These are the caracal, the serval, the small spotted cat and the African wild cat. The domestic cat (*Felis catus*), probably descended from a strain of *Felis lybica*, has become feral in certain areas and presents a serious ecological problem on Marion Island. Five specimens were introduced in 1949 to control the house mouse population and have multiplied alarmingly. They have seriously depleted the birdlife of the island. Furthermore on the mainland, where previously the African wild cat has been found near settlements, they have interbred with feral domestic cats and it is now difficult to find pure specimens near human habitation. It is possible that, because of this factor, the pure African wild cat may eventually disappear from this sub-region.

Caracal
Felis caracal
Rooikat

21

Caracal are unmistakable and are best known for the tuft of hair on the tips of their ears. Their speed and ferocity are well-known and, despite their relatively small size, with a weight of about 8-13 kg, they are formidable opponents to even big hunting dogs. The paws are relatively large and are fearful weapons, with long, sharp claws, the dew claws being particularly strong, sharp and heavy.

Sometimes erroneously known as lynx, the caracal are more robust and shorter-limbed animals than their closest relatives the servals. They are secretive, probably strictly crepuscular and nocturnal and are very rarely seen during the day. They are solitary except for short periods when mating. Although normally terrestrial, they are adept at tree-climbing. They sleep in appropriated burrows, hollow trees, thick bush or rock crevices.

Mainly silent, although they will spit and growl in anger and call their partners with a loud bark.

Caracal are relentlessly persecuted because of their reputation as stock killers. Where this does occur and even where mass killings have been recorded, the incidence of stock destruction is sufficiently scant to overlook these depredations and allow the animal to be left to its niche in nature. Caracal control the overpopulation of dassies. Only those caracal specifically identified as stock killers could be justifiably destroyed.

Their enemies are not known but the young are in danger from other predators. The female finds a secure position in deep cover, such as an antbear's hole or crevice in a large rock mass, which she lines with fur and feathers and gives birth to from one to six, but usually two to three, altricial kittens.

Food: Mammals, birds and reptiles comprise their food. They often leap into the air to take even the larger raptors such as the martial and tawny eagles, as well as guinea fowl and other bird species. Mammal food ranges from antelope as large as the bushbuck, monkeys and baboons, and as small as the smaller rodents, springhares and hares. Other prey include poisonous or non-poisonous snakes but their major food seems to be dassies. On occasion they also kill domestic stock and poultry. Fruit and grass is sometimes eaten.

Uncommon but widespread

Distribution: SOUTH AFRICA: *Transvaal*: Ben Alberts, Borokalano, Hans Merensky, Hans Strydom Dam, Klaserie, Kruger Park, Langjan, Lapalala, Londolozi, Mala Mala, Manyeleti, Messina, Nyala Ranch, Percy Fyfe, Pilanesberg, Roodeplaat Dam, Sabi-Sabi, Sabi-Sand, Timbavati, Umbabat/Motswari; *O.F.S.*: Erfenis Dam, Golden Gate, Soetdoring, Tussen-die-Riviere, Willem Pretorius; *Natal*: Giants Castle, Oribi Gorge, Royal Natal; *Cape*: Addo Elephant, Andries Vosloo, Aughrabies, Bontebok, De Hoop, Doornkloof, Gamkaberg, Gamkapoort, Goukamma, Hester Malan, Kalahari Gemsbok, Karoo, Keurboom, Kommandodrift, Langebaan, Mkambati, Mountain Zebra, Oviston, Robberg, Rolfontein, Salmon's Dam, Thomas Baines, Tsitsikamma Coastal, Tsitsikamma Forest, Vaalbos, Zuurberg.

NAMIBIA: Daan Viljoen, Eastern & Western Caprivi, Etosha, Hardap Dam, Kaudom, Mahonga, Naukluft, Skeleton Coast, Von Bach, Waterberg Plateau; BOTSWANA: Central Kalahari, Chobe, Gemsbok, Khutse, Mabuasehube, Makgadikgadi, Mashatu, Moremi, Nxai Pan; ZIMBABWE: Chete, Chewore, Chizarira, Gonarhezhou, Hwange, Malapati, Mana Pools, Matopos, Matusadona, Nyanga; MOZAMBIQUE: Gorongosa.

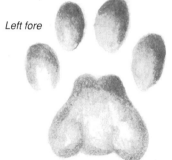

Left fore

Left hind

²/₃ *actual size*

SERVAL	
Gestation period: ± 70 days	
Young: one – six, usually two – three	
Mass: ♂ 13 kg, ♀ 10 kg.	
Length: ♂ 110 cm, ♀ 106 cm.	
Life expectancy: 17 years	

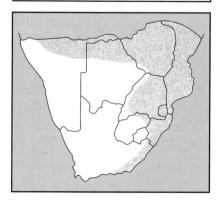

Serval
Felis serval
Tierboskat

22

The servals have largely disappeared from their original fairly wide range in the sub-region. They are now considered rare. They are elegant, long-legged, short-tailed cats, with large ears and attractive markings. The background colour of the pelt varies considerably within the populations of the sub-region but, whereas the markings also vary, the distinctive pattern type of these cats is unmistakable. They do not occur in desert or semi-desert areas as they are dependent on a permanent water supply and upon adequate shelter, such as high grass, undergrowth or reedbeds.

They are solitary, but sometimes pair or form family groups. Old burrows, thickets and rock crevices are used as lairs. They are nocturnal hunters but are also active in the day, particularly soon after sunrise or late afternoon. They are terrestrial animals but climb well and will take to trees for safety.

Their voice is a high-pitched repeated cry to call their mate. They snarl and spit when enraged and purr contentedly like domestic cats.

They are not very courageous and are sometimes preyed upon by larger predators. One to four, usually two to three, altricial kittens are produced in the lair.

Food: Mammalian prey ranging in size from mouse to oribi, including the lambs of larger antelope. Birds to guineafowl size are a favoured food and they often take avian prey on the wing, leaping high to snatch them out of the air. Other fare includes reptiles (snakes and lizards), fish, new grass and fruit. Sometimes take domestic poultry. Unlike most other cat species they will hunt in reeds and swampy area.

Rare but widespread

Distribution: SOUTH AFRICA: *Transvaal*: Hans Merensky, Klaserie, Kruger Park, Londolozi, Mala Mala, Manyeleti, Messina, Nyala Ranch, Roodeplaat Dam, Sabi-Sabi, Sabi-Sand, Suikerbosrand, Timbavati, Umbabat/Motswari; *Natal*: Giants Castle, Hluhluwe, Mkuzi, Ndumu, Oribi Gorge, Phinda, Royal Natal, St Lucia, Umfolozi.

NAMIBIA: Eastern & Western Caprivi, Etosha, Kaudom, Mahonga, Waterberg Plateau; BOTSWANA: Chobe, Makgadikgadi, Moremi, Nxai Pan; ZIMBABWE: Chete, Chewore, Chizarira, Gonarhezhou, Hwange, Malapati, Mana Pools, Matopos, Matusadona, Nyanga; MOZAMBIQUE: Gorongosa, Maputo Elephant.

Small spotted cat
Felis nigripes
Gekolde kat

23

Previously known as black-footed cats, a misleading name as only the pads are black, these small cats, associated with anthills wherein they sometimes live, are also known coloquially as 'miershooptier' (anthill tiger). These uncommon cats are smaller than, but not unlike, the African wild cat, but have both spots and stripes. They are intractable in temperament, particularly fierce for their small size and cannot be domesticated. There are two subspecies, a southern and a northern race. The southern race is more definitely marked with the marks a strong black, but this changes along the range northwards and the markings become less definite and washed out, with a rusty tinge.

They are nocturnal, secretive and little-known, react quickly to disturbance and make for cover at the first hint of danger. They are usually solitary but pair off temporarily to mate, sometimes with more than one male in attendance.

They are endemic to the sub-region and their habitat preference is open arid country with dense stands of grass or scrub. They appropriate disused antbear, springhaas and termite nest holes.

Their enemies are serval, caracal, leopard, honey badger and large owls. Kittens are taken by jackal, civets, genets, other small carnivores and snakes. One to two kittens are produced.

Food: Mice, spiders, shrews, lizards, insects and small birds.

Distribution: SOUTH AFRICA: *Transvaal*: Barberspan, *O.F.S.*: Golden Gate, Hendrik Verwoerd Dam, Maria Maroka, Soetdoring, Tussen-die-Riviere; *Cape*: Amalinda, Aughrabies, Bontebok, Doornkloof, Hester Malan, Kalahari Gemsbok, Kommandodrift, Mountain Zebra, Oviston, Rolfontein, Sandveld, Vaalbos.

NAMIBIA: Daan Viljoen, Hardap Dam; BOTSWANA: Central Kalahari, Gemsbok, Khutse, Mabuasehube, Makgadikgadi.

African wild cat
Felis lybica
Vaalboskat

24

Similar to but larger than the domestic cat, two sub-species are identified in the region. The animals from the more arid parts are more sandy and pale,

SMALL SPOTTED CAT

Gestation period: ± 65 days	
Young: one – two	
Mass: ♂ 1,6 kg, ♀ 1,1 kg.	
Length: ♂ 58 cm, ♀ 51 cm.	
Life expectancy: 13 years	

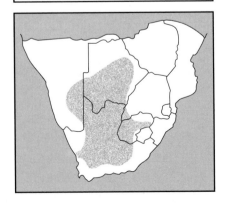

Left fore

Left hind

Actual size

AFRICAN WILD CAT

Gestation period: ± 58 days	
Young: two – three	
Mass: ♂ 5 kg, ♀ 4 kg.	
Length: ♂ 90 cm, ♀ 85 cm.	
Life expectancy: 12 – 15 years	

Left fore

Left hind

Actual size

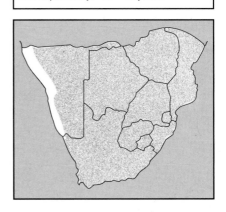

with reddish markings; those from wetter regions are blue-grey in colour with grey-black markings. The two intergrade and it is difficult to assign intermediate specimens to their sub-species. In central African rain forests all black specimens are recorded.

They are nocturnal, solitary and terrestrial in habit, moving late after sundown. They climb well if necessary, are cunning and difficult to trap. Unlike the small spotted cat they are easily tamed and become very affectionate. They have a wide habitat tolerance and are present in all areas except in deserts. They do, however, require some form of cover, such as rocks, scrub or thicket to form a den. Their voice is similar to the domestic cats; they growl, hiss, spit, mew and purr.

Enemies are as the small spotted cat. One to three altricial young are born in the den.

Food: Mice, then birds are the main fare. They also eat insects and other invertebrates, amphibia and wild fruit. They can be a danger to the young of stock and game animals and poultry.

Distribution: SOUTH AFRICA: *Transvaal*: Barberspan, Ben Alberts, Borokalano, Doorndraai Dam, Hans Merensky, Hans Strydom Dam, Klaserie, Kruger Park, Langjan, Lapalala, Londolozi, Mala Mala, Manyeleti, Nyala Ranch, Pilanesberg, Roodeplaat Dam, Sabi-Sabi, Sabi-Sand, Timbavati, Umbabat/Motswari; *O.F.S.*: Erfenis Dam, Golden Gate, Soetdoring, Tussen-die-Riviere, Willem Pretorius; *Natal*: Giants Castle, Hluhluwe, Mkuzi, Ndumu, Royal Natal, Phinda, St Lucia, Umfolozi; *Cape*: Andries Vosloo, Aughrabies, Botsalano, Doornkloof, Gamkaberg, Gamkapoort, Kalahari Gemsbok, Karoo, Kommandodrift, Langebaan, Mountain Zebra, Oviston, Rolfontein, Sandveld, Thomas Baines, Vaalbos, Zuurberg.

NAMIBIA: Daan Viljoen, Eastern & Western Caprivi, Etosha, Hardap Dam, Kaudom, Mahonga, Naukluft, Skeleton Coast, Von Bach, Waterberg Plateau; BOTSWANA: Central Kalahari, Chobe, Gemsbok, Khutse, Mabuasehube, Makgadikgadi, Mashatu, Moremi, Nxai Pan; ZIMBABWE: Chete, Chewore, Chizarira, Gonarhezhou, Hwange, Malapati, Mana Pools, Matopos, Matusadona, Nyanga; MOZAMBIQUE: Gorongosa, Maputo Elephant.

Fairly common and widespread

Bat-eared fox
Otocyon megalotis
Bakoorvos

25

These small canines are also known as Delalande's fox. They are probably named after the common Egyptian slit-faced bat (*Nycteris thebaica*), with its disproportionately large ears. The ears of the bat-eared fox are enormous, up to 13 cm long by 10 cm wide. The entire animal including its large bushy tail is only about 80 cm long. In the middle of the back is a hairy, glandular slit.

Left fore

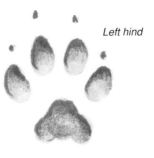

Left hind

³/₄ *actual size*

BAT-EARED FOX

Gestation period: ± 60 days
Young: two – six, usually three – four
Mass: 4 kg.
Length: 82 cm.
Life expectancy: 5,5 years

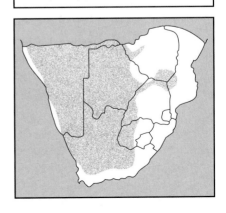

These inoffensive and ecologically valuable animals have been perse-cuted in ignorance and are victims of the sins of the destructive black-backed jackals, which are the object of hunts by farmers with their packs of dogs. As the dogs do not discriminate between fox, and jackal, the inoffen-sive bat-eared foxes and aardwolfs are frequently also killed.

Their preferred habitat is open semi-arid country, open areas of short grass and karoo scrub. They are absent from true desert and afforested areas. Their range seems to coincide closely with the range of their preferred food, the harvester termite (*Hodotermes mossambicus*). They are both noc-turnal and diurnal, but where they are persecuted they become exclusively nocturnal. Occasionally they will dig their own burrows, or occupy the aban-doned burrows of antbears and aardvark and, as they are good diggers, adjust the burrows to suit their requirements.

They are very playful and agile and have a colloquial name in Afrikaans - 'draaijakkals' (*draai* = turning) which describes both their play and avoid-ance capabilities. They are able to turn around very rapidly, even while running swiftly. They move in pairs and sometimes in small parties.

Enemies: Large birds of prey, spotted and brown hyaena. The bond between mates is very strong and they sometimes remain together for life. Five to six altricial pups are produced in holes in the ground.

Food: Mainly invertebrates, with insects (particularly ter-mites) being the highest component. Other invertebrates eaten include scorpions, centipedes, millipedes and sun spiders. Mice are also eaten as well as small snakes, lizards and wild fruit. Their remarkable hearing enables the animal to detect movement of prey underground, which is then dug up.

Distribution: SOUTH AFRICA: *Transvaal*: Hans Merensky, Kruger Park, Langjan, Messina, Nyala Ranch, Pilanesberg; *O.F.S.*: Soetdoring, Tussen-die-Riviere; *Cape*: Addo Elephant, Aughrabies, Bontebok, Doornkloof, Gamkaberg, Gamkapoort, Hester Malan, Kalahari Gemsbok, Karoo, Kommandodrift, Langebaan, Mountain Zebra, Oviston, Rocher Pan, Rolfontein, Vaalbos, Zuur-berg.

NAMIBIA: Daan Viljoen, Etosha, Hardap Dam, Kaudom, Mahonga, Naukluft, Skeleton Coast, Von Bach, Waterberg Plateau; BOTSWANA: Central Kalahari, Chobe, Gemsbok, Khutse, Mabuasehube, Makgadikgadi, Mashatu, Moremi, Nxai Pan; ZIMBABWE: Chizarira, Gonarhezhou, Hwange; MOZAMBIQUE: Gorongosa.

Very rare and localised

√ Wild dog
Lycaon pictus
Wildehond

26

Also known as Cape hunting dogs, these wolf-sized predators are inhabitants of savannah country. Although equally at home in open scrub woodland and semi-desert, they are absent from forests and desert. Sometimes they are referred to as 'painted wolves' and not without reason - with their remarkable patchwork hides, varying from individual to individual and the habit of hunting in packs, they are reminiscent of the wolves of northern climes.

They are very gregarious animals, forming packs of up to about 15 individuals, sometimes as many as 40. Packs of about 100 animals were recorded before the decline of game numbers. There is rarely any fighting within the packs and there is not much evidence of dominance by any one individual. They are generally strictly diurnal, most active in the early morning and late afternoon, but are also known to hunt on moonlit nights.

Hunting is by sight, which is preceded by considerable excitement accompanied by a loud bird-like twittering. The hunt consists of running tirelessly after the prey until it is too exhausted to continue, or is brought down by a bite to the groin and then torn to pieces. Larger prey, such as the wildebeest, is attacked while on the run. Pieces are torn off the animal and it is also disembowelled while still running.

Social concern is strong. Hungry dogs will lie around waiting for the young to eat before they do. They are generally tolerant of scavengers at their kills but have little tolerance for spotted hyaena which are generally driven off and often seriously mauled.

Vocalisation takes various forms. There is the well-known, far-carrying, soft hooo-hooo repeated up to six times, which is the rallying call to the pack; growling or a deep bark in the case of alarm; the twittering at the commencement of the hunt and just prior to the kill. The young yowl when lost or whine for food and the adults whine for appeasement.

Lions and leopards very occasionally take a dog but man is their most serious enemy. Young are taken by hyaenas. Cubs are born in grass-lined burrows often two females birthing together in the same burrow or nearby. From two to twelve altricial pups, usually about four, or

Common in the south, rarer northwards

WILD DOG

Gestation period: ± 70 days	
Young: two – sixteen, average seven	
Mass: 25 kg.	
Shoulder height: 68 cm.	
Life expectancy: 10 – 12 years	

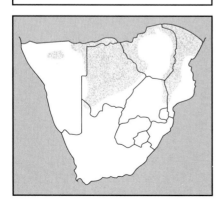

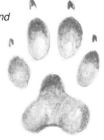

Left fore

Left hind

¹/₂ *actual size*

up to as many as sixteen, are born. They are fed on pre-masticated, regurgitated food.

Food: Every possible warm-blooded animal up to the size of a wildebeest is taken, including the young of larger animals. They will not eat carrion, however freshly killed.

Distribution: SOUTH AFRICA: *Transvaal*: Klaserie, Kruger Park, Londolozi, Mala Mala, Manyeleti, Sabi-Sabi, Sabi-Sand, Timbavati, Umbabat/Motswari; *Natal*: Hluhluwe, Umfolozi; *Cape*: Kalahari Gemsbok.

NAMIBIA: Eastern & Western Caprivi, Etosha, Kaudom, Mahonga; BOTSWANA: Chobe, Gemsbok, Makgadikgadi, Moremi, Nxai Pan; ZIMBABWE: Chete, Chewore, Chizarira, Gonarhezhou, Hwange, Mana Pools, Matusadona; MOZAMBIQUE: Gorongosa.

✓ Cape fox
Vulpes chama
Silwervos

27

Several fox species occur in Africa, but only one in this sub-region. The Afrikaans name is appropriate as the grizzling of the fur imparts a beautiful silvery sheen and the pelt is highly prized by indigenous people for use in traditional clothing. The widely used term 'silwerjakkals' (silver jackal) is incorrect as the animals are not jackals.

Cape fox are small, inoffensive and little-known animals which inhabit semi-desert scrub, open grassland, grassland with scattered thickets and the fynbos regions of the south western Cape. They are usually solitary and predominantly nocturnal. They have a strong body odour and mark their territory frequently with a strong-smelling secretion. They are strong diggers, digging their own burrows or appropriating those disused by antbears. They rest up in rocky crevices or burrows and favour the base of rocky kopjes.

Their voice is a high-pitched, but not loud, scream, followed by two or three yaps, a pair sometimes duetting together, with one howling and the other yapping. The yap is also an alarm call, especially by the female as a warning to her cubs. Will growl and spit when aggressive and, when excited, the tail is raised, with the degree of elevation indicative of the degree of excitement. Their predators are unknown. Three to five young are produced in their burrow.

Food: Mice, insects and other invertebrates, form the bulk of the food, with other components being birds and their eggs, small snakes and lizards, wild fruit and green grass.

Distribution: SOUTH AFRICA: *Transvaal*: Barberspan, Borokalano, Loskop Dam, Nyala Ranch, Pilanesberg, S A Lombard, Suikerbosrand; *O.F.S.*: Erfenis Dam, Hendrik Verwoerd Dam, Maria Maroka,

CAPE FOX

Gestation period: ± 52 days	
Young: three – five	
Mass: 3 kg.	
Length: 90 cm.	
Life expectancy: unknown	

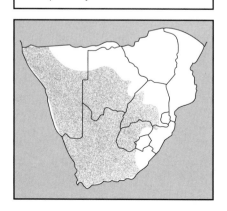

Left fore

Actual size

Left hind

Soetdoring, Tussen-die-Riviere, Willem Pretorius; *Natal*: Weenen; *Cape*: Addo Elephant, Amalinda, Aughrabies, Bontebok, Botsalano, De Hoop, Doornkloof, Gamkaberg, Gamkapoort, Goukamma, Hester Malan, Kalahari Gemsbok, Karoo, Keurboom, Kommandodrift, Langebaan, Mountain Zebra, Oviston, Rocher Pan, Rolfontein, Salmon's Dam, Sandveld, Vaalbos,

NAMIBIA: Daan Viljoen, Etosha, Hardap Dam, Naukluft, Skeleton Coast, Von Bach, Waterberg Plateau; BOTSWANA: Central Kalahari, Gemsbok, Khutse, Mabuasehube.

JACKALS

Two jackal species are found in the sub-region. These are the black-backed and the side-striped. The former is the more aggressive and destructive of the two. Both are particularly susceptible to infection by rabies. The two species overlap to only a small extent across the common borders of their occurrence, except in the east where there is a fairly large overlap.

Black-backed jackal

Canis mesomelas

Rooijakkals

28

The black-backed jackal is marginally smaller than the side-striped jackal and weighs up to 8 kg. The Afrikaans name rooijakkals (red jackal) is very descriptive, particularly in winter, as the animals develop a rich reddish colour to their flanks and sides, usually darker on their flanks and on top of the muzzle.

The black-backed jackal is a problem animal which is relentlessly hunted by farmers and 'problem animal hunting units' with packs of dogs. Unfortunately these dogs also attack the inoffensive side-striped jackal, the bat-eared fox and the aardwolf, tearing them to pieces. It is not difficult to understand the farmer's attitude when confronted with their stock depredation, but it may be short-sighted to indiscriminately destroy these animals as they have a distinct place in keeping the balance of nature. Their indiscriminate destruction has, in some places, resulted in the proliferation of their small prey such as the mongoose, which in turn feeds upon the eggs of the burrow-nesting South African shelduck. Consequently this is seriously diminishing the occurrence of this attractive arid-country bird.

They have wide habitat tolerance, favouring drier bushveld and savannah grassland types, but not forests. Mainly diurnal, they may also be active at night. Their preferred shelters are disused antbear holes and crevices in piles of boulders, favouring these more substantial places to simple thick underbrush. Predators are mainly lion, leopard and large birds of prey. Will defend themselves savagely when attacked.

Vixens give birth to up to ten, usually four to six, altricial pups using antbear burrows and other holes.

BLACK-BACKED JACKAL

Gestation period: ± 64 days

Young: two – ten, usually five – seven

Mass: ♂ 8 kg, ♀ 7 kg.

Length: ♂ 115 cm, ♀ 100 cm.

Life expectancy: 10 years, up to 14 years in captivity

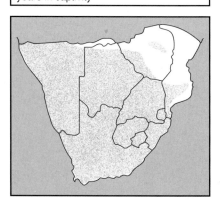

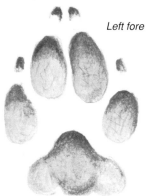

Left fore

³/₄ actual size

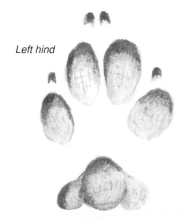

Left hind

Food: They actively hunt smaller prey such as small ante- lope and the very young of larger antelope as well as hares, mongooses, springhaas and a large variety of rodents. Will take young sheep and goats, a wide variety of snakes, lizards, insects, mainly crickets, beetles, and grasshoppers, as well as other invertebrates such as sun spiders, spiders and scorpions. Vegetable matter is also eaten. They are renowned carrion scavengers.

Distribution: SOUTH AFRICA: *Transvaal*: Barberspan, Ben Alberts, Ben Lavin, Borokalano, Doorndraai Dam, Hans Merensky, Hans Strydom Dam, Klaserie, Kruger Park, Langjan, Lapalala, Londolozi, Mala Mala, Messina, Nyala Ranch, Nylsvley, Percy Fyfe, Pilanesberg, Roodeplaat Dam, Rustenburg, Sabi-Sabi, Sabi- Sand, S A Lombard, Suikerbosrand, Timbavati, Umbabat/Motswari; *O.F.S.*: Bloemhof Dam, Erfenis Dam, Golden Gate, Maria Maroka, Soetdoring, Tussen- die-Riviere, Willem Pretorius; *Natal*: Giants Castle, Hluhluwe, Mkuzi, Ndumu, Oribi Gorge, Phinda, Royal Natal, St Lucia, Umfolozi; *Cape*: Addo Elephant, Amalinda, Andries Vosloo, Aughrabies, Botsalano, Doornkloof, Gamkaberg, Gamkapoort, Hester Malan, Kalahari Gemsbok, Kommandodrift, Langebaan, Mkambati, Mountain Zebra, Oviston, Rolfontein, Sandveld, Vaalbos, Zuurberg.

Common locally

NAMIBIA: Daan Viljoen, Etosha, Hardap Dam, Kaudom, Naukluft, Skeleton Coast, Von Bach, Waterberg Plateau; BOTSWANA: Central Kalahari, Chobe, Gemsbok, Khutse, Mabuasehube, Makgadikgadi, Mashatu, Moremi, Nxai Pan; ZIMBABWE: Gonarhezhou, Hwange, Matopos; MOZAMBIQUE: Maputo Elephant.

Side-striped jackal
Canis adustus
Witkwasjakkals

Unlike the black-backed, the colour of the side-striped is rather cryptic and nondescript. They weigh up to 10 kg and are marginally larger than the black-backed jackal. There is a broad white tip to the tail.

They tend to prefer more thickly wooded, well- watered country but not forests and are generally noctur- nal, but may be encountered soon after sunrise and before sunset and occasionally at other times in the day. Preferred shelters are the same as those of the black-backed jackal.

Side-striped jackals are timid animals, easily over- come by dogs. Their predators are similar to those of the black-backed jackal: Lion, leopard, large birds of prey. Vixens give birth to up to ten, usually four to six, altricial pups in holes or antbear burrows.

Rare but widespread

Food: Mainly vegetable matter, such as wild fruit, figs and

SIDE-STRIPED JACKAL

Gestation period: ± 60 days

Young: one – four

Mass: ♂ 9,5 kg, ♀ 8,5 kg.

Length: 110 cm.

Life expectancy: 10 – 12 years

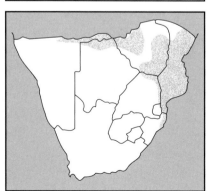

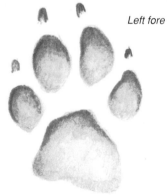

Left fore

Actual size

Left hind

peanuts (agricultural products). The next highest preferences are various small mammals, mainly rodents and also hares. Birds, small snakes and lizards, insects and carrion but to a far lesser extent than the other species.

Distribution: SOUTH AFRICA: *Transvaal*: Hans Merensky, Klaserie, Kruger Park, Londolozi, Mala Mala, Manyeleti, Messina, Nylsvley, Sabi-Sabi, Sabi-Sand, Timbavati, Umbabat/Motswari; *Natal*: Mkuzi, Ndumu, Phinda, St Lucia.

NAMIBIA: Eastern & Western Caprivi, Etosha, Kaudom, Mahonga; BOTSWANA: Chobe, Moremi; ZIM-BABWE: Chete, Chewore, Chizarira, Mana Pools, Matopos, Matusadona; MOZAMBIQUE: Gorongosa, Maputo Elephant.

OTTERS

Only two otters are represented in the sub-region. Both are easily distinguished from the other: The cape-clawless otter lacks evident claws, having only vestigial 'finger nails'. The spotted-necked otter (*Lutra maculicollis*) has well-developed claws. As the two Afrikaans names indicate, the cape-clawless otter is the larger animal. The spotted-necked otter is proportionally longer and slimmer. Only the Cape clawless otter is dealt with here.

Cape clawless otter

Aonyx capensis

Groototter

30

Cape-clawless otters are diurnal, but will occasionally hunt on moonlit nights. On warmer days they are inactive in the hotter times. Largely aquatic, they spend considerably more time out of the water than does the spotted-necked otter. When leaving the water to dry themselves they vigorously shake their heads, then their entire body, then actively dry themselves in sand or on short grass. They sun themselves in all manner of postures, often comical. Their movements are generally slow and sinuous, but will gallop in an undulating motion. They are extremely playful, often sliding down mud-banks into the water and playing endlessly with pebbles and sticks. Their fingers are very dextrous and sensitive and they will hunt their prey by feeling in the mud. They prefer muddy to clear water, unlike the spotted-necked otter, which must have clear water.

They use their holts (or resting places) in the heat of the day and at night. These are usually dry holes, under rocks, in reed beds or dry erosion gullies. They are often found in river estuaries and even out to sea, sometimes wandering far from water at night in search of a new habitat.

Their predators are crocodiles in the water; the young are sometimes taken by pythons. Little is known of their reproduction, but it would seem that one, rarely two, altricial young are produced in the usual holts.

Right
fore

Right
hind

$^1/_3$ actual size

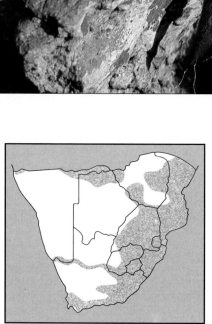

CAPE CLAWLESS OTTER

Gestation period: ± 67 days	
Young: one, rarely two	
Mass: ♂ 14 kg, ♀ 12 kg.	
Length: 130 cm.	
Life expectancy: 15 years	

Common in suitable habitat

Food: They eat fish, crabs, frogs, reptiles, small and medium-sized mammals, waterfowl, the eggs of ground nesting birds and of crocodiles. In the marine environment they eat fish, crabs, octopi and other molluscs. They become problem animals when they take domestic free-range ducks. The cape-clawless otter generally consumes its fish from the head to the tail and the spotted-necked otter from the tail to the head.

Distribution: SOUTH AFRICA: *Transvaal*: Borokalano, Doorndraai Dam, Hans Strydom Dam, Klaserie, Kruger Park, Londolozi, Mala Mala, Nylsvley, Pilanesberg; *O.F.S.*: Erfenis Dam, Golden Gate, Soetdoring, Tussen-die-Riviere, Willem Pretorius; *Natal*: Giants Castle, Mkuzi, Oribi Gorge, Royal Natal, St Lucia, Umfolozi; *Cape*: Addo Elephant, Amalinda, Andries Vosloo, Aughrabies, Bontebok, De Hoop, Doornkloof, Gamkapoort, Goukamma, Karoo, Keurboom, Kommandodrift, Mkambati, Oviston, Rolfontein, Sandveld, Thomas Baines, Tsitsikamma Coastal, Tsitsikamma Forest, Vaalbos, Zuurberg.

NAMIBIA: Eastern & Western Caprivi, Etosha, Kaudom, Mahonga; BOTSWANA: Chobe, Mashatu, Moremi; ZIMBABWE: Chizarira, Matopos, Nyanga; MOZAMBIQUE: Gorongosa, Maputo Elephant.

Honey badger
Mellivora capensis
Ratel

31

Honey badgers are sometimes referred to as Ratels in English text. They are small animals, well known for their courage, ferocity, treachery and tenacity. The pelt and skin is thick, moving loosely on the body. It is difficult for the jaws of a predator to get a hold of it, allowing the badgers to twist around and get at the attacker. The forepaws are armed with powerful, long, curved claws, dorsally broad and ventrally sharp like a knife, with sharp tips. The back claws lack the knife edge and are, instead, hollowed out underneath. The forepaws are used to dig for prey even in the hardest ground.

They are aggressive and attack without provocation. Like polecats, when stressed will ooze a foul-smelling excretion from a pair of anal glands. The exudation clings persistently. They are not prone to use this defence mechanism and prefer to attack. They may also feign death if in a no-way-out situation. Will put up a spirited defence against even lion. Any animal foolish enough to tackle one of these powerful little creatures is likely to find itself in serious trouble.

Badgers are nocturnal animals but do venture out in the daytime. Their habitat requirements seem to be cosmopolitan excluding true desert. They are found even in urban and suburban situations. They live in burrows

HONEY BADGER

Gestation period: ± 200 days	
Young: one – two	
Mass: 11 kg.	
Length: 95 cm.	
Life expectancy: up to 24 years in captivity	

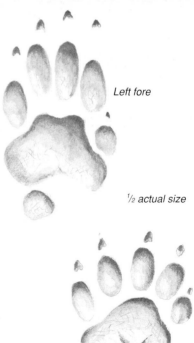

Left fore

¹/₂ *actual size*

Left hind

which have either been appropriated and adapted or dug, as well as in rocky crevices. Honey badgers move with a slow, rolling, sinuous gait with nose close to the ground, snuffling for their prey.

Their vocalisation is a soft 'haarr-haarr' when disturbed and they will growl, grunt or yowl loudly when under stress.

Enemies are not known as few animals are bold enough to tackle them. Potential predators are also repelled by the anal discharge. They produce one to two young in their burrows.

Food: They are problem animals when they take to raiding poultry. Wire netting is no barrier to their powerful claws and they are inclined to kill far more than they need. They are also an apiarist's nightmare, tearing up the beehives to get to comb and honey. In the wild they are reported to allow themselves to be led by some of the honeyguide bird species to nests. This is, however, as yet unproven. Their other fare comprises carrion, young game animals, including young antelope, rodents, ground birds, eggs, snakes, lizards and tortoises, fish, crabs, frogs, insects, spiders and their favourite, the scorpions, which they prefer above other live food. They also eat fruit, berries and tubers.

Distribution: SOUTH AFRICA: *Transvaal*: Doorndraai Dam, Hans Merensky, Hans Strydom Dam, Klaserie, Kruger Park, Langjan, Londolozi, Mala Mala, Manyeleti, Messina, Nylsvley, Pilanesberg, Sabi-Sabi, Sabi-Sand, Timbavati, Umbabat/Motswari; *Natal*: Hluhluwe, Mkuzi, Ndumu, Phinda, St Lucia, Umfolozi; *Cape*: Aughrabies, Goukamma, Hester Malan, Kalahari Gemsbok, Karoo, Keurboom, Robberg, Tsitsikamma Coastal, Tsitsikama Forest, Zuurberg.

NAMIBIA: Daan Viljoen, Eastern & Western Caprivi, Etosha, Hardap Dam, Kaudom, Mahonga, Naukluft, Skeleton Coast, Von Bach, Waterberg Plateau; BOTSWANA: Central Kalahari, Chobe, Gemsbok, Khutse, Mabuasehube, Makgadikgadi, Mashatu, Moremi, Nxai Pan; ZIMBABWE: Chete, Chewore, Chizarira, Gonarhezhou, Hwange, Malapati, Mana Pools, Matopos, Matusadona, Nyanga; MOZAMBIQUE: Gorongosa, Maputo Elephant Park.

Common and widespread

STRIPED POLECAT

Gestation period: ± 36 days

Young: one – five, usually one – three

Mass: ♂ 950 g, ♀ 700 g.

Length: ♂ 63 cm, ♀ 60 cm.

Life expectancy: 5,5 years

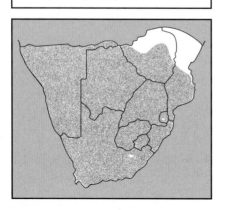

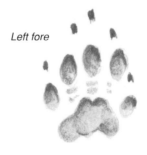

Left fore

Left hind

Actual size

POLECATS AND WEASELS

Two closely related species of the sub-family Mustelinae occur in the sub-region, both of which use an evil-smelling chemical defence to deter their predators. Only the striped polecat is dealt with here.

Striped polecat
Ictonyx striatus
Stinkmuishond

32

Also known as the white-naped weasel, these small nocturnal carnivores are easily identified and also distinguished from the only other similar animals, the much smaller striped weasels, by their bold longitudinal black-and-white striped shaggy coats, shaggy black and white tails, pointed heads with white below the ears and sometimes a patch of white on the forehead. The front claws are long and strong.

Because of their nocturnal habits they are mostly seen only as traffic casualties on roadways. They are usually solitary, emerging after dark from their burrows - either self-dug or appropriated - or from rock crevices, under piles of stones, barns or stables. They are terrestrial but climb well if they have need to do so. Their habitat preference is wide, from desert conditions to light forest, and they are found throughout the sub-region, but are nowhere very common. The movement is a fast trot, with sudden stops to cast about to sniff out possible prey. The tail is held horizontal when the animal is on the trot, but vertical if stressed. If they are cornered they will aggressively face the danger, erecting the hair of their coats and tails. Under extreme provocation they will turn their rear to the aggressor and forcibly eject a foul-smelling, clinging, offensive secretion. They are easily tamed and will not use their chemical weapon readily, relying rather on barking and growling to make their point. They are preyed upon by the smaller predators, but their defence proves an efficient deterrent to all but the hungriest. They produce one to five, usually two to three, altricial young.

Food: Principal food is insects and mice, but will readily take reptiles, birds, frogs, crabs, spiders, scorpions, sun spiders and centipedes.

Distribution: SOUTH AFRICA: *Transvaal*: Barberspan, Blyde River Canyon, Borokalano, Doorndraai Dam, Hans Merensky, Hans Strydom Dam, Klaserie,

Very rare and localised

Left fore

Left hind

Actual size

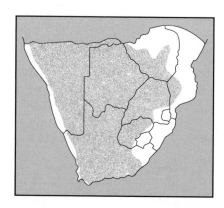

SMALL-SPOTTED GENET

Gestation period: ± 70 days

Young: one – four, usually one – three

Mass: 2 kg.

Length: 95 cm.

Life expectancy: 14 years

Kruger Park, Langjan, Londolozi, Loskop Dam, Manyeleti, Messina, Nyala Ranch, Nylsvley, Ohrigstad Dam, Percy Fyfe, Pilanesberg, Roodeplaat Dam, Rustenburg, Sabi-Sabi, Sabi-Sand, S A Lombard, Sterkspruit, Timbavati, Umbabat/Motswari; *O.F.S.*: Bloemhof Dam, Erfenis Dam, Hendrik Verwoerd Dam, Maria Maroka, Soetdoring, Tussen-die-Riviere, Willem Pretorius; *Natal*: Hluhluwe, Itala, Loteni, Mkuzi, Ndumu, Oribi Gorge, Phinda, Umfolozi, Weenen; *Cape*: Amalinda, Andries Vosloo, Aughrabies, Bontebok, Botsalano, De Hoop, Doornkloof, Gamkaberg, Gamkapoort, Goukamma, Hester Malan, Kalahari Gemsbok, Karoo, Kommandodrift, Langebaan, Mountain Zebra, Oviston, Salmon's Dam, Sandveld, Thomas Baines, Tsitsikamma Coastal, Tsitsikamma Forest, Vaalbos, Zuurberg.

SWAZILAND: Pongola; NAMIBIA: Daan Viljoen, Eastern & Western Caprivi, Etosha, Hardap Dam, Kaudom, Naukluft, Skeleton Coast, Von Bach, Waterberg Plateau; BOTSWANA: Central Kalahari, Chobe, Gemsbok, Khutse, Mabuasehube, Makgadikgadi, Mashatu, Moremi, Nxai Pan; ZIMBABWE: Chete, Chewore, Chizarira, Gonarhezhou, Hwange, Malapati, Matopos, Matusadona, Nyanga; MOZAMBIQUE: Gorongosa, Maputo Elephant.

GENETS & CIVETS

Two genet and two civet species, relatives of the mongooses and not the cats as some of their colloquial names suggest, are found in the subregion. The small-spotted genet is distinguished by the presence of a dorsal crest and a white-tipped tail; the large-spotted genet has no crest and a broad black tip to the tail. The names are misleading, as the spots on the small-spotted genet are not always smaller than those of the large-spotted genet. The alternative name, rusty-spotted genet, used for the large-spotted genet is also misleading, as the spots are not always rusty and the spots of the small-spotted genet are sometimes reddish in colour.

Their larger relatives, the civets, are widespread throughout tropical Africa. One of the two species of civet which occur here, the tree civet *Nandinia binotata* extends into the subregion, but only in the afforested areas of eastern Zimbabwe. It is a rarely seen, nocturnal, arboreal animal of lowland forest and evergreen riverine and is not dealt with in this work.

Small-spotted genet
Genetta genetta
Kleinkolmuskejaatkat

33

Also known as the common genet, these are strictly nocturnal mainly terrestrial animals which will readily climb trees. Their range, which extends into Europe and the Middle East, is wider than that of the large-spotted genet, which ranges northwards, only up to, and not beyond, the Sahara Desert. Their preferred habitat is woodland and drier areas of grassland with adjoining or mosaic woodland. For this reason they are absent from densely afforested wet areas and true desert. This contrasts with the habitat preference of *G. tigrina* which prefers wetter conditions.

For their resting place they generally use underbrush cover, piles of boulders, hollow logs, sometimes holes in trees and in the ground, such as antbear burrows. They do not modify the burrows in any way. When stressed they secrete an evil-smelling musk from anal glands. They have a varied vocalisation, an 'uff-uff-uff' contact call, a growling in excitement, whining and mewing in mating and squeaking in pain.

Enemies are serval, caracal, leopard, badger and large owls. Kittens are endangered by jackals, civets, owls and snakes. The young are born in holes in trees and in the burrows and rock piles. One to four, usually two to three, altricial young are produced. Young twitter constantly in the nest when the mother is absent.

Common in the south, widespread

Food: Small animals from hare-size, birds up to guineafowl size, eggs, reptiles, insects, spiders, sun spiders, scorpions, millipedes, sometimes crabs, freshwater snails, sometimes fruit and carrion. Can become a problem animal with poultry.

Distribution: SOUTH AFRICA: *Transvaal*: Ben Alberts, Ben Lavin, Blyde River Canyon, Doorndraai Dam, Klaserie, Kruger Park, Lapalala, Londolozi, Loskop Dam, Mala Mala, Manyeleti, Messina, Nyala Ranch, Nylsvley, Pilanesberg, Sabi-Sabi, Sabi-Sand, S A Lombard, Suikerbosrand, Timbavati, Umbabat Motswari; *O.F.S.*: Bloemhof Dam, Erfenis Dam, Soetdoring, Tussen-die-Riviere, Willem Pretorius; *Cape*: Addo, Aughrabies, Bontebok, De Hoop, Doornkloof, Gamkaberg, Gamkapoort, Goukamma, Hester Malan, Kalahari Gemsbok, Karoo, Keurboom, Kommandodrift, Langjan, Mountain Zebra, Salmon's Dam, Sandveld, Thomas Baines, Vaalbos, Zuurberg.

NAMIBIA: Daan Viljoen, Etosha, Hardap Dam, Kaudom, Mahonga, Von Bach, Waterberg Plateau, BOTSWANA: Central Kalahari, Gemsbok, Mabuasehube, Makgadikgadi, Mashatu, Nxai Pan; ZIMBABWE: Gonarhezhou, Malapati, Matopos, Hwange.

Large-spotted genet

Genetta tigrina

Rooikolmuskejaatkat

34

Similar in form to G. *genetta*, the ears are shorter and rounder and the behaviour is similar, but their preferred habitat is swampy, watered and forested areas. Their range is the higher rainfall of the eastern areas of the subregion. The forests of the southern Cape and the macchia zone of the Cape. They are very active and, even with their short legs, are able to move very swiftly. They will sit on their hind legs, balancing with their tails, to survey the area. They are nocturnal and normally solitary, but occasionally pairs have been noted moving together. Like the small-spotted genet, they will, under stress, secrete a heavy, evil-smelling musky odour from their anal glands.

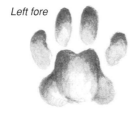

Left fore

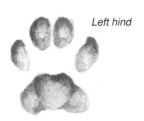

Left hind

Actual size

LARGE-SPOTTED GENET

Gestation period: ± 65 days
Young: one – four, usually one – three
Mass: 2 kg.
Length: 100 cm.
Life expectancy: 13 years

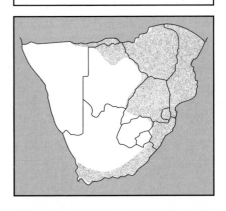

Common in the north, rare in the south

Their enemies, reproduction and food are similar to those of the small-spotted genet.

Distribution: SOUTH AFRICA: *Transvaal*: Ben Lavin, Blyde River Canyon, Doorndraai Dam, Hans Merensky, Klaserie, Kruger Park, Langjan, Lapalala, Londolozi, Loskop Dam, Mala Mala, Manyeleti, Nylsvley, Pilanesberg, Roodeplaat Dam, Rustenburg, Sabi-Sabi, Sabi-Sand, S A Lombard, Sterkspruit, Timbavati, Umbabat Motswari; *Natal*: Hluhluwe, Kenneth Stainbank, Mkuzi, Ndumu, Oribi Gorge, Phinda, St Lucia, Umfolozi; *Cape*: Addo Elephant, Amalinda, Andries Vosloo, Bontebok, De Hoop, False Bay, Gamkaberg, Gamkapoort, Goukamma, Keurboom, Mkambati, Robberg, Salmon's Dam, Sandveld, Thomas Baines, Tsitsikamma Coastal, Tsitsikamma Forest; SWAZILAND: Pongola.

BOTSWANA: Chobe, Moremi, NAMIBIA: Eastern & Western Caprivi; ZIMBABWE: Chete, Chewore, Chizarira, Gonarhezhou, Malapati, Mana Pools, Matopos, Matusadona, Nyanga, Hwange; MOZAMBIQUE: Gorongosa, Maputo Elephant.

✓ Civet

Civettictis civetta

Afrikaanse siwet

35

Also known as the African civet, these viverrids are considerably larger than the genets, weighing about five times as much. Their larger size and distinctive markings at once distinguish the two genera. They are nocturnal, terrestrial animals, with a preferred habitat of fairly well-watered grassland and forest, with the highest populations occurring where surface water is plentiful. They are generally solitary and move around with a purposeful walk with head held low. They tend to react to danger by relying on camouflage and will only 'explode' out of cover when approached too closely. They erect their spectacular mane, which is longest on the rump and the root of the tail, as a defensive gesture and tend to move sideways to show off their display. Almost completely silent in the wild, their vocalisation when evidenced is a growling and a spitting when angry, a scream when in combat and a closed 'ha-ha-ha' for contact, or a spitting cough, when confronted, accompanied by a high jump on all four feet with erection of the mane.

The musk secreted as a territorial marking has been used in the past as an ingredient in the perfume trade. It has now largely been replaced by synthetic substitutes.

Their enemies probably include leopard and caracal. The young are at

Left fore

Actual size

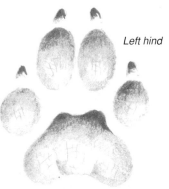

Left hind

CIVET	
Gestation period: ± 68 days	
Young: one – four, usually two – three	
Mass: 10 kg.	
Length: 130 cm.	
Life expectancy: 14 years	

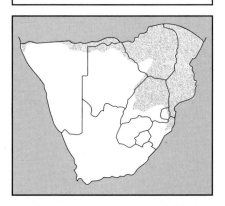

Relatively common in suitable habitat

risk from genets, smaller cats, hyaenas, mongooses and pythons. One to four, usually two to three, young are born in the animal's shelters which may be the disused burrow of an antbear or in a pile of rocks

Food: The civet is omnivorous, eating mainly insects and also wild fruit, rodents, reptiles, birds, amphibians, millipedes and centipedes, fish and grass. They are known to take the calves of small antelope and also domestic cats.

Distribution: SOUTH AFRICA: *Transvaal*: Hans Merensky, Hans Strydom Dam, Klaserie, Kruger Park, Londolozi, Mala Mala, Manyeleti, Messina, Nyala Ranch, Pilanesberg, Sabi-Sabi, Sabi-Sand, Timbavati, Umbabat/Motswari; *Natal*: Mkuzi, Ndumu, Phinda; *Cape*: Langjan, Zuurberg.

NAMIBIA: Eastern & Western Caprivi, Etosha, Kaudom, Mahonga, Waterberg Plateau; BOTSWANA: Chobe, Mashatu, Moremi; ZIMBABWE: Chete, Chewore, Chizarira, Gonarhezhou, Hwange, Malapati, Mana Pools, Matopos, Matusadona, Nyanga; MOZAMBIQUE: Gorongosa, Maputo Elephant.

Suricate
Suricata suricatta
Stokstertmeerkat

36

Like the civets and genets, the suricates of the mongoose family are viverrids, and are only very distantly related to the cats. They are burrowing animals with front claws strong, long and curved, ideally adapted for digging. Their ears are guarded by a fold of the posterior and superior ridges, which close while the animals dig. They characteristically sit upright on their haunches, balanced by their tail, which is thick at the base, tapering to the tip. Sometimes a dozen or more are observed in this pose which is a charming and common sight on the bare african veld. While in this stance their heads turn from side to side intently scanning the heavens for the approach of an aerial predator. On sensing danger they bark shrilly and the whole pack dives into their burrows for cover. After a while one after the other will reappear and cautiously cast around for danger and then once again take up their stance, after which they will, one at a time, drop onto their forefeet and begin to forage. They turn over stones and scratch in the earth for their favoured insect fare.

Their preferred habitat is the more open arid parts of the country, where there is a hard stony soil substrate. They extend into the macchia zone in the south west, but not in the true coastal desert of Namibia. They are endemic

SURICATE OR MEERKAT

Gestation period: ± 75 days	
Young: two – five, usually two – three	
Mass: 700 g.	
Length: 50 cm.	
Life expectancy: 10 years	

Left fore

Left hind

Actual size

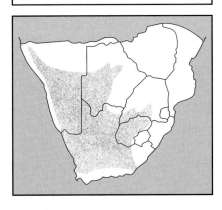

Suricate in typical pose

to the subregion, with a short extension into south eastern Angola.

Colonies consist of up to 30 or more animals living in self-dug or appropriated burrows. These are extensive and with many entrances. The detritus, from their burrowing, piles up at the entrances and the warrens are marked by these characteristic mounds. Burrows are sometimes shared with other animals such as ground squirrels and springhaas and are sometimes abandoned because of vermin or lack of food in the immediate area. Their range is usually not much more than up to 200 metres from the burrows. Burrows are occasionally expropriated from ground squirrels, who also share these with the yellow mongoose. When the suricates have moved off they may be reoccupied.

They have a wide variety of voice, with a short growl as a contact call, whining and grunting in contentment, a sharp and repeated 'kroo' when annoyed and a repeated sharp bark when in danger from avian predators, or a staccato bark as a warning against terrestrial predators.

Their predators are African wild cat, servals, jackals, badgers (which dig them out of the burrows) and larger birds of prey. They have litters of two to five, usually two to three, altricial young.

Food: Insects and other invertebrates, bird's eggs, reptiles including poisonous snakes, snails.

Distribution: SOUTH AFRICA: *Transvaal*: S A Lombard, Suikerbosrand; *O.F.S.*: Erfenis Dam, Hendrik Verwoerd Dam, Maria Maroka, Soetdoring, Tussen-die-Riviere, Willem Pretorius; *Cape*: Addo Elephant, Amalinda, Andries Vosloo, Aughrabies, Doornkloof, Hester Malan, Kalahari Gemsbok, Karoo, Kommandodrift, Mountain Zebra, Oviston, Rocher Pan, Rolfontein, Sandveld, Thomas Baines, Vaalbos.

NAMIBIA: Daan Viljoen, Etosha, Hardap Dam, Naukluft, Von Bach; BOTSWANA: Central Kalahari, Gemsbok, Khutse, Mabuasehube.

MONGOOSES

There are eleven mongooses in the sub-region, five of which are not dealt with in this account and are as follows:

The rare Meller's mongoose *Rhynchogale melleri*, occurs through central, eastern and western Zimbabwe, central and southern Mozambique and south eastern Transvaal Lowveld. It is similar to the white-tailed mongoose, but is considerably larger and blacker in colour, at least from the mid back to the base of the tail. The tail is not white.

The bushy-tailed mongoose *Bdeogale crassicauda* is found in northern Zimbabwe and northern Mozambique. In the field it looks black, but only the limbs and tail are jet black, with the rest of the body grizzled.

The rare and little-seen Selous mongoose *Paracynictis selousi*, is found throughout Zimbabwe; western and southern Mozambique; northern, north western and eastern Transvaal; Natal: northern Zululand. It is similar to, but smaller and darker than, the white-tailed mongoose. The tail is white-tipped only towards the tip, whereas the tail of the white-tailed mongoose is white for more than two thirds of its length. Their enemies are, dependent upon the size of the mongoose, the larger predators, including black-backed jackal, and larger raptors.

The two little-known, large grey mongoose *Herpestes ichneumon*, also known as the Egyptian mongoose, and small grey mongoose *Galerella pulverulenta*, also known as the Cape grey mongoose, are not included.

The grizzled, pepper & salt appearance of many of the species are as a result of annulated guard hairs, the rings alternating black or dark grey and whitish or buff or reddish, which, lying in juxtaposition, create the overall grizzled effect.

Yellow mongoose

Cynictis penicillata
Witkwasmuishond, geelmuishond

37

Also known outside the sub-region as the bush-tailed mongoose, with the name 'yellow mongoose' also ascribed to a mongoose (*Herpestes ochracae*) from north east Africa. The names given to this mongoose are to a certain extent misleading. The northern Botswana animals are smaller, grey in colour and the tails are shorter and not tipped with white, unlike the southern specimens which are a rich tawny yellow in colour and have white-tipped tails.

These are terrestrial, predominantly diurnal animals, which are also known to be active at night. They are common in parts of their range, gregarious by nature and form colonies of twenty, up to fifty or even more

YELLOW MONGOOSE

Gestation period: ± 60 days	
Young: two – four, usually two	
Mass: 800 g.	
Length: 58 cm.	
Life expectancy: 12 years	

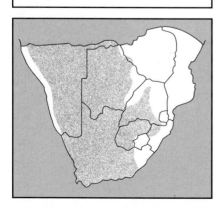

Left fore

Left hind

Actual size

animals. Solitary burrows have been found housing single, pairs or several together. They sometimes share burrows with ground squirrels, suricates or other mongoose species. Colonies are begun in abandoned springhaas, suricate or antbear holes and can be situated in rock piles, among the roots of acacia and other trees, or in the open. These are extensively restructured and enlarged. Their extensive burrowing sometimes create mounds so large that their more extensive warrens are sometimes located even above the surrounding ground level. As they are colonial animals they are dangerous carriers and spreaders of rabies.

Like the suricates, they will also stand upright for long periods on their hind legs, surveying the countryside. Their preferred habitat is open plains with scanty grass and bush cover as well has rocky, hilly country.

Predators are as in the introductory paragraph. Two to four, usually two to three, young are born in the burrows, which are kept clean and bare.

Food: They are mainly insect eaters, predominantly ants and termites, as well as grasshoppers, crickets and beetles. Spiders, sun spiders, centipedes, small ground birds, mice, reptiles - mainly lizard species, but also some snakes and frogs are eaten. Free-range chickens are sometimes taken.

Distribution: SOUTH AFRICA: *Transvaal*: Barberspan, Blyde River Canyon, Doorndraai Dam, Loskop Dam, Nylsvley, Ohrigstad Dam, Roodeplaat Dam, Rustenburg, S A Lombard, Sterkspruit, Suikerbosrand; *O.F.S.*: Bloemhof Dam, Erfenis Dam, Hendrik Verwoerd Dam, Maria Maroka, Soetdoring, Tussen-die-Riviere, Willem Pretorius; *Cape*: Amalinda, Andries Vosloo, Aughrabies, Bontebok, Botsalano, De Hoop, Doornkloof, Gamkaberg, Gamkapoort, Goukamma, Hester Malan, Kalahari Gemsbok, Karoo, Keurboom, Kommandodrift, Langebaan, Mkambati, Mountain Zebra, Oviston, Robberg, Rocher Pan, Rolfontein, Salmon's Dam, Sandveld, Thomas Baines.

NAMIBIA: Daan Viljoen, Eastern & Western Caprivi, Etosha, Hardap Dam, Kaudom, Mahonga, Naukluft, Von Bach, Waterberg Plateau; BOTSWANA: Central Kalahari, Chobe, Gemsbok, Khutse, Mabuasehube, Makgadikgadi, Moremi, Nxai Pan; ZIMBABWE: Hwange.

Slender mongoose

Galerella sanguinea

Swartkwasmuishond

38

The animals vary considerably in colour and are normally a grizzled yellow-brown to rich red-brown, with a characteristic long black-tipped tail. Animals from central and northern Namibia were formerly regarded as a separate species. These lack the grizzled colour of the animals from the rest of the region and are dark brown with a broad band of very dark brown or black from the nose to the tip of the tail. In the field they appear to be black.

In the sub-species from northern Kaokoveld in Namibia and southern Angola, the upper parts are chestnut-red or yellowish-orange, the under

SLENDER MONGOOSE

Gestation period: unknown	
Young: usually two	
Mass: ♂ 630 g, ♀ 550 g.	
Length: ♂ 60 cm, ♀ 55 cm.	
Life expectancy: unknown	

Left fore

Actual size

Left hind

parts are lighter and the long tail is characteristically broadly tipped with long black hair.

These slender little animals are sinuous in their movements. When running for cover they carry their tails vertically, or will flick them up to the vertical position just before diving into cover. Are inclined to use open roads and tracks to hunt, moving in and out of the bordering grass and, for this reason, are often seen. When curious they will sit up on their haunches to have a look around. They hole up in a large variety of covers, varying from rock crevices, to burrows, to termitaria or to hollow trees. They keep a close watch out for hovering raptors. Very quiet animals, their contact call is a soft 'hoo'.

They are solitary, terrestrial animals, but climb well, taking to trees in times of danger. They are mainly diurnal, appearing late in the morning and will not move at all in cold or overcast weather. Are found in a wide habitat ranging from deserts to rain forest, on the plains, or in the mountains. They favour close proximity to water and will live in close association with man, even living under the floors of outbuildings.

Predators are as in the introductory paragraph. The young are born in any of the variety of hiding places mentioned and usually two are produced at a time.

Food: Insects, mainly grasshoppers, lizards, rodents, small birds, bird's eggs and wild fruit.

Distribution: SOUTH AFRICA: *Transvaal*: Barberspan, Ben Alberts, Ben Lavin, Blyde River Canyon, Borokalano, Doorndraai Dam, Hans Merensky, Hans Strydom Dam, Klaserie, Kruger Park, Langjan, Lapalala, Londolozi, Loskop Dam, Mala Mala, Manyeleti, Messina, Nyala Ranch, Nylsvley, Ohrigstad Dam, Percy Fyfe, Pilanesberg, Roodeplaat Dam, Rustenburg, Sabi-Sabi, Sabi-Sand, S A Lombard, Sterkspruit, Suikerbosrand, Timbavati, Umbabat Motswari; *O.F.S.*: Bloemhof Dam, Erfenis Dam, Maria Maroka, Soetdoring, Tussen-die-Riviere, Willem Pretorius; *Natal*: Hluhluwe, Itala, Kenneth Stainbank, Mkuzi, Ndumu, Oribi Gorge, Phinda, St Lucia, Umfolozi, Weenen; *Cape*: Botsalano, Vaalbos.

SWAZILAND: Pongola; NAMIBIA: Daan Viljoen, Eastern & Western Caprivi, Etosha, Hardap Dam, Kaudom, Mahonga, Von Bach, Waterberg Plateau; BOTSWANA: Central Kalahari, Chobe, Gemsbok, Khutse, Mabuasehube, Makgadikgadi, Mashatu, Moremi, Nxai Pan; ZIMBABWE: Chete, Chewore, Chizarira, Gonarhezhou, Malapati, Mana Pools, Matopos, Matusadona, Nyanga, Hwange; MOZAMBIQUE: Gorongosa, Maputo Elephant.

Common and widespread

White-tailed mongoose

Ichneumia albicauda

Witstertmuishond

39

White-tailed mongooses are among the larger and heavier of the mongooses of the region. The hindquarters appear higher and heavier than the forequar-

WHITE-TAILED MONGOOSE

Gestation period: unknown	
Young: two – three	
Mass: ♂ 5 kg, ♀ 4 kg.	
Length: ♂ 110 cm, ♀ 100 cm.	
Life expectancy: 12 years	

Left fore

²/₃ *actual size*

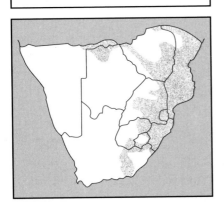

Left hind

ters because of the much longer hair on the hindquarters. The guard hair is much longer and sparser than the underfur, giving the animals a shaggy appearance. The tail hair is longer at the base, becoming shorter towards the tip. The tail is white in appearance, but the individual hairs have an annulated ring of grey and are broadly white-tipped. The limbs are almost jet-black.

They are nocturnal, not being in evidence until well after sunset and are commonly seen after dark with their white tails standing out in the headlights of a car. If disturbed they freeze and in danger will erect the body and tail hair. Because of their long hair they appear to be short-legged, but this is incorrect and they are capable of good speed over short distances. They do not sit up on their haunches, as do some of the other mongooses, but will find a suitable rock or stump upon which to raise themselves and rest their forepaws if they want to look around. They do not climb trees.

They are not gregarious, are normally solitary, in pairs or small family groups. Although they can dig they do not make their own burrows but use any available deserted burrow or under rocks. They are savannah species and are not found in desert, semi-desert or forest areas.

Predators are as in the introductory paragraph. One to three young are born in the burrow.

Food: They eat mainly insects (preferring termites), followed by frogs, mice, reptiles (including fairly large poisonous snakes), wild fruit, birds and earthworms.

Distribution: SOUTH AFRICA: *Transvaal*: Blyde River Canyon, Borokalano, Doorndraai Dam, Hans Merensky, Hans Strydom Dam, Klaserie, Kruger Park, Langjan, Londolozi, Loskop Dam, Mala Mala, Manyeleti, Nylsvley, Ohrigstad Dam, Roodeplaat Dam, Sabi-Sabi, Sabi-Sand, Sterkspruit, Timbavati, Umbabat/Motswari; *O.F.S.*: Erfenis Dam, Golden Gate, Hendrik Verwoerd Dam, Maria Maroka, Soetdoring, Tussen-die-Riviere, Willem Pretorius; *Natal*: Giants Castle, Hluhluwe, Itala, Kamberg, Kenneth Stainbank, Loteni, Mkuzi, Ndumu, Oribi Gorge, Royal Natal, St Lucia, Umfolozi, Weenen; *Cape*: Addo Elephant, Amalinda, Andries Vosloo, Mkambati, Oviston.

NAMIBIA: Mahonga; BOTSWANA: Moremi; ZIMBABWE: Chewore, Gonarhezhou, Mana Pools, Nyanga, Hwange, Matopos; MOZAMBIQUE: Gorongosa, Maputo Elephant.

Fairly common and widespread

Water mongoose
Atilax paludinosus
Kommetjiegatmuishond

40

Water mongooses are also known elsewhere as marsh mongooses. Their colour varies considerably, ranging from almost black through to reddish-

WATER MONGOOSE

Gestation period: unknown	
Young: one – two	
Mass: 3,5 kg.	
Length: ♂ 90 cm, ♀ 80 cm.	
Life expectancy: 11 years	

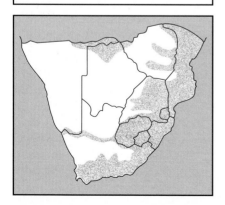

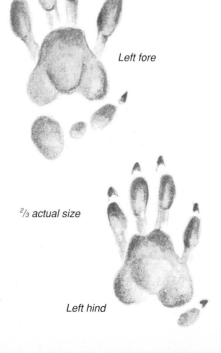

Left fore

²/₃ actual size

Left hind

brown. Coats are generally grizzled, very evident in some and scarcely evident in others. The hair feels harsh if stroked. The head is generally heavier and broader than the other mongooses and the muzzle shorter. The digits on the feet tend to splay when the animal walks, which facilitates walking on muddy places.

These highly excitable animals are crepuscular in habit. They are active from very early morning to about 08h30 and late afternoon to about 19h00. They are very sensitive to, and distressed by, strong light. They are terrestrial and normally solitary, with adult females sometimes accompanied by juveniles. They are good swimmers and their habitat is close to water: the fringes of rivers, lakes, dams and swamps. They need heavy cover and hole up in dense reeds, under large piles of vegetation, or any sheltered place near to water. They will not settle down well in captivity and are in a frenzy if approached.

Predators are as in the introductory paragraph. One or two young are produced in the burrow.

Food: Major food is frogs, frog's eggs and crabs. Small rodents, insects (particularly water insects and their larvae) and fish.

Rare and restricted by habitat

Distribution: SOUTH AFRICA: *Transvaal*: Blyde River Canyon, Doorndraai Dam, Hans Merensky, Hans Strydom Dam, Klaserie, Kruger Park, Langjan, Loskop Dam, Mala Mala, Manyeleti, Nylsvley, Ohrigstad Dam, Pilanesberg, Roodeplaat Dam, Sabi-Sabi, Sabi-Sand, Timbavati, Umbabat/Motswari; *O.F.S.*: Erfenis Dam, Golden Gate, Hendrik Verwoerd Dam, Tussen-die-Riviere, Willem Pretorius; *Natal*: False Bay, Hluhluwe, Itala, Mkuzi, Ndumu, Oribi Gorge, Phinda, St Lucia, Umfolozi; *Cape*: Aughrabies, De Hoop, Doornkloof, Goukamma, Karoo, Keurboom, Kommandodrift, Langebaan, Mkambati, Oviston, Robberg, Rolfontein, Salmon's Dam, Tsitsikamma Coastal, Tsitsikamma Forest; SWAZILAND: Pongola.

NAMIBIA: Hardap Dam; ZIMBABWE: Gonarhezhou, Malapati, Matopos; MOZAMBIQUE: Gorongosa.

Banded mongoose

Mungos mungo

Gebande muishond

41

Clearly distinguished from all other mongooses by the conspicuous banding across the lower back. The coats and tails are grizzled and the tapering tail is black- or brown-tipped. The coat is harsh to the touch when stroked.

Gregarious, strictly diurnal animals except they may venture out on moonlit nights. Live in packs numbering up to 30 or more animals, maintaining contact by making a twittering sound when they scatter to forage.

BANDED MONGOOSE

Gestation period: ± 60 days	
Young: two – six	
Mass: 1,5 kg.	
Length: 58 cm.	
Life expectancy: 11 years	

Right fore

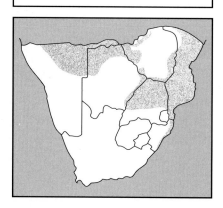

Right hind

Actual size

When danger threatens will twitter stridently, upon which the rest of the pack 'freezes', with individuals rising on their back legs, balancing with their tails on the ground to survey the area. They will then quietly slip away to the safety of their burrows or into the thicket. In severe danger they will immediately dive into cover which was previously located.

Have a wide habitat tolerance, but absent from desert or semi-desert areas, preferring open woodland and underbush, with fallen logs, other fallen woodland detritus and termitaria. They are terrestrial, but good tree climbers if in danger, are able to swim, have keen senses and are able to detect underground prey. They are not dependent upon water, receiving all necessary moisture from their diet. Dens are disused burrows of such animals as antbears and springhares, which are not permanent dwellings. They may occupy them for a few days to a few weeks and then abandon them.

Predators are as in the introductory paragraph. Two to six young are born in the burrow.

Common and
widespread

Food: The main fare is invertebrates, such as millipedes, centipedes, spiders and scorpions, insects such as beetles and their larvae, grasshoppers, crickets and termites. Carrion is eaten, wild fruit, snakes, lizards and frogs. Any creatures, such as toads which have a noxious skin secretion, or caterpillars with poisonous spines, are rolled around in the sand until the offensive matter is removed.

Distribution: SOUTH AFRICA: *Transvaal*: Ben Lavin, Blyde River Canyon, Borokalano, Doorndraai Dam, Hans Merensky, Hans Strydom Dam, Klaserie, Kruger Park, Langjan, Lapalala, Londolozi, Loskop Dam, Mala Mala, Manyeleti, Messina, Nyala Ranch, Nylsvley, Ohrigstad Dam, Pilanesberg, Sabi-Sabi, Sabi-Sand, Sterkspruit, Timbavati, Umbabat/Motswari; *Natal*: False Bay, Hluhluwe, Kenneth Stainbank, Mkuzi, Phinda, Ndumu, St Lucia; *Cape*: Zuurberg.

NAMIBIA: Eastern & Western Caprivi, Etosha, Kaudom, Mahonga, Von Bach, Waterberg Plateau; BOTSWANA: Central Kalahari, Chobe, Makgadikgadi, Mashatu, Moremi, Nxai Pan; ZIMBABWE: Chewore, Gonarhezhou, Hwange, Malapati, Mana Pools, Nyanga; MOZAMBIQUE: Gorongosa, Maputo Elephant.

√ Dwarf mongoose

Helogale parvula

Dwergmuishond

42

They are the smallest of the region's mongooses, being only about 40 cm overall, with tails about half that length. Their colour is a very dark brown almost black. The upper-parts are grizzled.

DWARF MONGOOSE

Gestation period: ± 52 days

Young: two – seven, usually two – four

Mass: 260 g.

Length: 38 cm.

Life expectancy: 6 years

Left fore

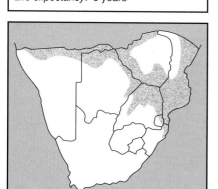

Left hind

Actual size

They are diurnal, seldom venturing out until the sun is well-risen and will not come out in cold, rainy or overcast weather. They are terrestrial but will clamber on fallen logs. If in danger they will climb trees, descending head first. They are gregarious animals, forming troops of up to 10 or more, scattering away from their burrows to forage, but keeping contact with a constant twittering. Under threat they will growl with arched back and raised neck hair, which grows louder as the threat increases. They are playful, sun-loving animals and engage in much mutual grooming.

Dwarf mongoose prefer open woodland with associated grassland. They choose hard stony ground with termitaria, rock heaps, stone piles and tree and shrub detritus. Are generally found in burrows in termitaria, but may dig their own, which run deep underground. Not found in desert, semi-desert or forest, they are associated with stony, broken ground. The permanent burrows are marked by the presence of much fecal deposit.

Predators are as in the introductory paragraph. Two to seven, usually two to four, young are born. Young females sometimes kidnap young, taking them to other burrows. If the mother does not retrieve them they die of hunger.

Common and widespread

Food: The main food is insect species, beetles and their larvae being preferred, also termites, crickets and grasshoppers. Spiders and centipedes, lizards and snakes, even large poisonous snakes are subdued and eaten by the pack, mice, snails and bird's eggs, both of which are precipitated through the back legs against a hard object to break them. Slimy creatures or furry caterpillars are cleaned in sand and furry animals are skinned.

Distribution: SOUTH AFRICA: *Transvaal*: Ben Alberts, Ben Lavin, Blyde River Canyon, Borokalano, Doorndraai Dam, Hans Merensky, Hans Strydom Dam, Klaserie, Kruger Park, Langjan, Londolozi, Loskop Dam, Mala Mala, Manyeleti, Messina, Nyala Ranch, Ohrigstad Dam, Percy Fyfe, Sabi-Sabi, Sabi-Sand, Sterkspruit, Timbavati, Umbabat/Motswari; *Natal*: False Bay, Mkuzi, Ndumu, Phinda, St Lucia.

NAMIBIA: Eastern & Western Caprivi, Etosha, Kaudom, Mahonga, Waterberg Plateau; BOTSWANA: Chobe, Moremi, Nxai Pan; ZIMBABWE: Chete, Chewore, Chizarira, Hwange, Mana Pools, Matopos, Matusadona; MOZAMBIQUE: Gorongosa, Maputo Elephant.

ANTBEAR

Gestation period: ± 7 months	
Young: one, rarely two	
Mass: 50 kg.	
Shoulder height: 60 cm.	
Life expectancy: 18 years	

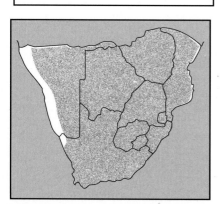

Left fore

¹/₂ actual size

Left hind

Antbear

Orycteropus afer

Erdvark

43

These curious animals, also known as 'Aardvark' have a very wide distribution, but are nowhere common. They are rarely seen due to their nocturnal and secretive habit, but do come out in the day after a cold night to sun themselves, lying on an anthill and sleeping soundly. They block the entrance to the occupied hole with sand and leave a small air vent. They are believed to wander very widely and dig many temporary burrows, which is of benefit to many other tenants, but they return to the central burrow in which the young are born. These burrows can be extensive, with a ramification of interleading tunnels with terminal chambers and several entrances. Other temporary holes are a nuisance to farmers as they can cause serious damage to vehicles.

They appear to have a very wide habitat tolerance, being found in virtually all terrain with termite populations. They are believed to be solitary, with any pairing probably only for the purpose of mating. Where there are large populations, however, several may be found sleeping together in one burrow.

Their burrows are the home of many species of fauna, indeed some are entirely dependent on the antbear's burrow, such as the South African shelduck *Tadorna cana*.

Although they have remarkable scent ability, they do not see well and crash into trees and wade through bushes when an easier path nearby could have been taken. They pay scant attention to bright lights, showing that their eyesight plays little part in their physiology. Their ears are long, relatively hairless and are folded back to exclude sand when in their burrows.

Their tongues, which can be in excess of 30cm long, are used to capture large numbers of ants and termites. This fare, including much sand is transferred almost directly into the gizzard, which grinds the ants and sand down. The jaws have curious teeth, each of which have as many as 1000 to 1500 dentine-filled tubes cemented together into a tooth, hence the name of their order, 'tubulidentata'. Why they have teeth is not known as these play virtually no part in the mastication of their food. Their claws are strong, the front claws especially so, and are equipped for digging and breaking up the rock-hard termitaria.

Their voice is a snorting grunt whilst on the move, grunting before entering their holes and a loud bleating in fright or terror.

Enemies are lion, leopard, cheetah, hyaena, hunting dog and pythons. One altricial young, rarely two, is produced in the burrow.

Food: Antbears are myrmacophagous animals. Their food is almost exclusively ants or termites. They are, however, recorded as eating beetle larvae and vegetable matter, in the form of melons. Small mice have been discovered in their digestive tracts.

Distribution: SOUTH AFRICA: *Transvaal*: Barberspan, Ben Alberts, Ben Lavin, Borokalano, Doorndraai Dam, Hans Merensky, Klaserie, Kruger Park, Langjan, Lapalala, Londolozi, Mala Mala, Manyeleti, Messina, Nyala Ranch, Nylsvley, Percy Fyfe, Pilanesberg, Roodeplaat Dam, Rustenburg, Sabi-Sabi, Sabi-Sand, S A Lombard, Suikerbosrand, Timbavati, Umbabat Motswari; *O.F.S.*: Erfenis Dam, Soetdoring, Tussen-die-Riviere, Willem Pretorius; *Natal*: Hluhluwe, Mkuzi, Ndumu, Phinda, St Lucia, Umfolozi; *Cape*: Addo Elephant, Andries Vosloo, Aughrabies, Bontebok, Botsalano, Doornkloof, Gamkaberg, Gamkapoort, Hester Malan, Kalahari Gemsbok, Karoo, Kommandodrift, Mountain Zebra, Rolfontein, Sandveld, Thomas Baines, Vaalbos, Zuurberg.

NAMIBIA: Daan Viljoen, Eastern & Western Caprivi, Etosha, Hardap Dam, Kaudom, Mahonga, Naukluft, Skeleton Coast, Von Bach, Waterberg Plateau; BOTSWANA: Central Kalahari, Chobe, Khutse, Makgadikgadi, Mashatu, Moremi, Nxai Pan; ZIMBABWE: Chete, Chewore, Chizarira, Gonarhezhou, Hwange, Malapati, Mana Pools, Matopos, Matusadona, Nyanga; MOZAMBIQUE: Gorongosa, Maputo Elephant.

Common in suitable habitat, widespread

√ African elephant
Loxodonta africana
Olifant

44

The adult male African elephant is the bulkiest and heaviest of all land mammals. The weight of a prime bull can be as much as 6000 kg with the heaviest recorded just over 6500 kg. African elephant sub-species occur throughout east and west central Africa, where only the forest elephant is significantly different, but only as regards its smaller size and darker hide. The elephants of the Far East are markedly different both in shape and temperament.

Although there is only one sub-species in southern Africa, the habitat tends to influence their behavioral patterns and even their appearance.

There are two major extremes of habitat in which elephant are found in our sub-region - the arid and waterless Kaokoveld and the dense forests of Knysna. By far the largest proportion of elephants is, however, found in bushveld country. The desert elephants of the waterless Kaokoveld need just as much food and water to survive as the other elephants. They are extremely careful in their eating, stripping off only the food needed, as if aware of how delicately balanced is nature in their arid and sparsely vegetated habitat. The Kaokoveld elephants are tall, scrawny and tough. The possible extinction of these endangered desert elephants holds severe threat

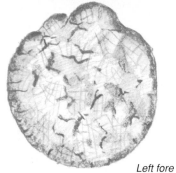

Left fore

$^{1}/_{10}$ *actual size*

ELEPHANT

Gestation period: ± 22 months	
Young: one, rarely two	
Mass: ♂ 5 750 kg, ♀ 3 800 kg.	
Shoulder height: 280 cm.	
Tusks: length: max. ♂ 3,4 m, ♀ 0,75 mass: max. ♂ 100 kg, ♀ 30 kg.	
Life expectancy: 65 years	

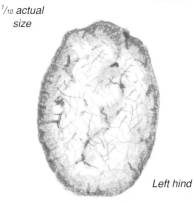

Left hind

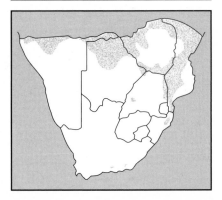

for the ecology of the Kaokoveld. They are the only creatures able to keep open the watering points in the shifting sands and if they disappear so will much of the fauna of the area dependent upon this water.

Elephants are generally placid, but can be extremely dangerous if threatened or when they are in season. There are two aggressive behavioral patterns: If the animal is not serious about its intent, but just wishes to assert itself or show its dominance, it may make a mock charge, trumpeting loudly, with the trunk probably extended and the ears flapping. If, however, the animal is intent on mischief, then the trunk may be rolled up for protection or left dangling, the ears are laid flat against the head and the tusks pointed directly at the quarry. The charge made is deadly in its silence.

Undeniably the glory, yet the downfall of this magnificent beast, is the bulk and quality of the ivory of its tusks. The heaviest recorded pair were an incredible almost 200 kg, recorded from an animal from central Africa. The record in our region are no more than 90 kg.

Elephants live to about 70 years, or sometimes slightly longer, with their age-span strictly controlled by their dentition. They have only six pairs of molars, with two in use at a time. As one pair is used they move forward along the jaw and are worn and splintered away by constant chewing and the roots are finally absorbed. That pair is replaced by the next which are longer and wider. Finally, when all six teeth on each side have been worn away, the elephant has attained old age. Now unable to chew its food, it dies from a lack of nutrition.

The female differs from the male in having a slightly more angular and prominent forehead and a slightly straighter back. Tusks are generally smaller, although this becomes noticeable only when compared to tusks of older bulls. The entire weight of the massive skull and tusks is carried by the forelegs which are larger than the back legs. The front feet are more rounded than the hind, which are smaller and more oval. When the elephant flaps its ears the blood supply in the heavy concentration of blood vessels near to the surface on the back of the ears cools, lowering the body heat of the animal.

Elephants do not go off to die in special 'elephant graveyards' as popular legend would have it. Their remains do not litter the veld as the scavengers, large and small, ultimately remove all evidence even of this the largest of all land animals. Due to their large size they do not have predators in the normal sense, but poaching and culling have taken their toll of the African elephant.

These social animals are ruled by a matriarchy. The senior cow in the family takes care of the needs of the family. Sometimes families join to form herds, but the larger bulls join the herd only when the cows are in oestrus, leaving again after their task is done.

Bulls rarely fight over the cows and may mate with several in the herd.

A single pinkish coloured, hairy calf is produced and rarely a twin. A clear place near water is chosen for the birthing and sometimes other females attend to guard the mother. The young are at risk and are strictly guarded by the mother and herd.

Food: Elephants are strict vegetarians: tree-bark and roots, leaves, softer branches, grass, and fruit is eaten, such as the baobab fruit and acacia pods.

Common and widespread

They consume prodigious quantities of food. Where man has interfered with nature and elephant populations permitted to expand unnaturally, the vegetation has suffered severely. Large branches are ripped off and the tender components eaten, smaller trees are sometimes toppled to make their tender crowns available, even the huge succulent, soft-pulp baobab tree trunks are chewed around until they topple and the entire tree is eventually consumed.

Distribution: SOUTH AFRICA: *Transvaal*: Klaserie, Kruger Park, Londolozi, Mala Mala, Manyeleti, Pilanesberg, Sabi-Sabi, Sabi-Sand, Timbavati, Umbabat/Motswari; *Natal*: Hluhluwe, Phinda; *Cape*: Addo Elephant.

NAMIBIA: Eastern & Western Caprivi, Etosha, Kaudom, Mahonga, Skeleton Coast; BOTSWANA: Chobe, Mashatu, Moremi, Nxai Pan; ZIMBABWE: Chete, Chewore, Chizarira, Gonarhezhou, Hwange, Malapati, Mana Pools, Matusadona; MOZAMBIQUE: Gorongosa, Maputo Elephant.

DASSIE

Four types of dassie occur in the sub-region and only the rock dassie is dealt with in detail.

The other three are: the Kaokoveld rock dassies (*Procavia welwitschii*) which have a limited distribution in this sub-region, from the northern limit of the occurrence of *P. capensis*, N.E. of Windhoek in Namibia, northwards across the Angolan border and with the western limit at about the longitude of the Waterberg Plateau, but not along the coastal strip. They are very similar to *P. capensis*, differing mainly in the coarser coat, the presence of pale, off-white patches behind and at the bases of the ears and, in particular, the pale-yellow or white of the dorsal spot, which is black in *P. capensis*. Habits of both species seem to be very similar.

The yellow-spotted rock dassies (*Heterohyrax brucei*) occur in the northern Transvaal, eastern Botswana and Zimbabwe. Very like *P. capensis* in appearance, they are identical in habit. Their main distinguishing features are the whitish underparts and the presence of conspicuous white or off-white patches above the eyes, whereas the *P. capensis* may have pale patches which are never white and at best inconspicuous. The name derives from the yellowish to ochre colour of the hair on the dorsal glandular patch, which in the *P. capensis* is black. Often both species are found coexisting happily together in the same rock niches, but each maintaining their own burrows.

The tree dassies (*Dendrohyrax arboreus*) have longer hair than rock dassies, giving them a woolly appearance. The hairs on the dorsal gland are white or off-white and the long tactile hairs evident on all the other dassies are not present. They are found in the lowland evergreen forests of the east coast and use holes in trees, the thick foliage of trees and matted creepers as their resting places.

Rock dassie

Procavia capensis

Klipdas *or* **Klipdassie**

45

The closest relatives of these ubiquitous little animals are the elephants and dugongs and they were formerly included together with these two large animals in the same super order. They are mainly diurnal animals, living in rocky places, but do, however, occupy road culverts and even abandoned antbear holes if population pressure denies them a rocky home. This problem may cause their migration, sometimes for considerable distances, to the next suitable habitat.

They are not very active and lie around sunning themselves for most of the time. Shy and fleet of foot, their padded paws allow them to climb very steep smooth surfaces and trees. They heap and huddle together in their dens and the nose is brought into close contact with the dorsal glandular spot, suggesting that it is a means of identification. The erection of the hair of the gland has been identified as being related to both aggression and sub-mission. Scattered through their coat are long tactile hairs, which apparently are used to align the animals in their burrows and rocky galleries.

Aggression is accompanied by the baring of teeth and growling, which usually sends the other submissive animal scurrying away. Vocalisation is varied, with snorts, squeals, wails, grunts and growls. The most usual being the sharp danger warning bark of the dominant male or female. They have long sharp triangular incisor teeth which are effective defence weapons.

They are prolific breeders and man's destruction of their predators, such as the black eagle, other large raptors, caracal, leopards and jackal, has caused severe population increase and attendant veld destruction. Other enemies are African wild cats, civets and large snakes. The litters number one to six, usually two to three. The young are precocial, and are able to move nimbly about within a day of birth.

Right fore

Actual size

Right hind

ROCK DASSIE

Gestation period: ± 230 days

Young: one – six, usually two – three

Mass: 4 kg.

Length: 50 cm.

Life expectancy: 12 years

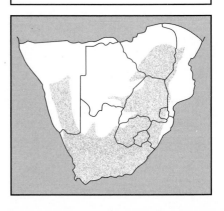

Common in restricted
habitat

Food: They are vegetarian and eat a wide variety of plant food. They are both browsers and grazers and are able to safely ingest highly poisonous plants. Insects and lizards sometimes form part of the diet.

Distribution: SOUTH AFRICA: *Transvaal*: Ben Alberts, Ben Lavin, Blyde River Canyon, Borokalano, Doorndraai Dam, Hans Merensky, Hans Strydom Dam, Klaserie, Kruger Park, Langjan, Lapalala, Londolozi, Loskop Dam, Messina, Nyala Ranch, Ohrigstad Dam, Percy Fyfe, Pilanesberg, Roodeplaat Dam, Rustenburg, Sabi-Sabi, Sabi-Sand, S A Lombard, Sterkspruit, Timbavati, Umbabat/Motswari; *O.F.S.*: Erfenis Dam, Golden Gate, Hendrik Verwoerd Dam, Maria Maroka, Tussen-die-Riviere, Willem Pretorius; *Natal*: Giants Castle, Itala, Kamberg, Kenneth Stainbank, Loteni, Oribi Gorge, Royal Natal, St Lucia, Umfolozi; *Cape*: Addo Elephant, Amalinda, Andries Vosloo, Aughrabies, Bontebok, De Hoop, Doornkloof, Gamkaberg, Gamkapoort, Goukamma, Hester Malan, Karoo, Keurboom, Kommandodrift, Mkambati, Mountain Zebra, Oviston, Robberg, Rocher Pan, Rolfontein, Sandveld, Thomas Baines, Tsitsikamma Coastal, Tsitsikamma Forest, Vaalbos, Zuurberg.

SWAZILAND: Pongola; NAMIBIA: Daan Viljoen, Hardap Dam, Naukluft; BOTSWANA: Mashatu; ZIMBABWE: Gonarhezhou, Hwange, Malapati, Matopos, Nyanga

RHINOCEROS

Two species are found in Africa, the square-lipped (white rhino) and the hook-lipped (black rhino). All rhino species world-wide are, or have been, on the brink of extinction due to the value of their horns. Strict conservation measures in southern Africa have reversed this, but even today these giants of the veld are threatened. The Zambesi valley, which is the last stronghold of significantly large numbers of black rhino, has been the scene of very extensive poaching activity. The existence of these rhino is further threatened by the projected damming of the Zambesi at the Mupata gorge, which would flood the Mana Pools area.

The spurious value placed upon the horns is as a result of the supposed aphrodisiac properties of the powdered horn in the Far East and the immense price paid by wealthy Yemenis for the horn, from which is made the hafts of important ceremonial weapons.

The horn consists of a tight hard mass of tubular filaments, similar to hair, and is an outgrowth of the skin which is not attached to the bone of the skull. Both animals have two tandem horns. The white rhino is the larger of the two species.

√White rhinoceros
Ceratotherium simum
Witrenoster

46

The name White Rhino comes from the original name 'Wydt Rhino' which referred to the width of its mouth. The maximum mass of the white rhino is about 2300 kg for the male and 1600 kg for the female. The maximum length of its front horn, which is considerably larger than the rear horn, is about 150 cm. The major differing characteristics between the two species are as follows:

The white rhino (more correctly the square-lipped rhinoceros) has a square upper lip, which is necessary for its grazing habit. The black rhino (more correctly the hook-lipped rhinoceros) has a prehensile hook-shaped upper lip.

The white rhino is the larger animal. Its colour is lighter grey, the black rhino's colour is dark grey.

The white rhino is more placid, and consequently less dangerous, than its bad-tempered cousin.

The calf of the white rhino usually precedes its mother when walking and the black rhino calf usually follows after its mother.

Both species have very poor vision, but their sense of hearing and scent

WHITE RHINOCEROS

Gestation period: ± 450 days	
Young: one	
Mass: ♂ 2 300 kg, ♀ 1 600 kg.	
Shoulder height: 180 cm.	
Horns: ♂ length: max., 150 cm., aver. 95 cm. ♀ longer & thinner	
Life expectancy: 40 years	

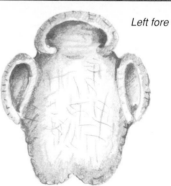

Left fore

⅙ actual size

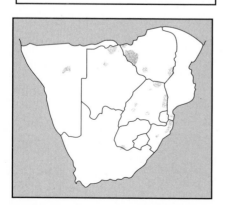

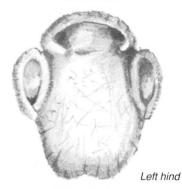

Left hind

is very good. When running or trotting the white rhino holds its head near to the ground, unlike the black rhino which runs with its head held high. The males of both species will do battle with competitors for the females and battles between males of the black rhino are, in particular, very savage affairs.

The white rhino favours grassy woodland, with short grass and plenty of water, woodland being necessary to provide shade. It is very fond of a mud wallow.

Apart from man there are no predators of the white rhino. A single calf is produced which could be taken by the larger predators if they dared the wrath of the mother.

Food: The staple food is grass, particularly fairly short grass, which it crops off to very close to the ground almost to a lawn-like appearance.

Common in restricted habitat

Distribution: SOUTH AFRICA: *Transvaal*: Ben Alberts, Klaserie, Kruger Park, Lapalala, Londolozi, Loskop Dam, Mala Mala, Manyeleti, Nyala Ranch, Pilanesberg, Sabi-Sabi, Sabi-Sand, Timbavati; *O.F.S.*: Bloemhof Dam, Tussen-die-Riviere, Willem Pretorius; *Natal*: Hluhluwe, Itala, Mkuzi, Ndumu, Phinda, Umfolozi, Weenen; *Cape*: Botsalano, Rolfontein, Thomas Baines, Vaalbos.

NAMIBIA: Waterberg Plateau; BOTSWANA: Chobe, Moremi; ZIMBABWE: Gonarhezhou, Hwange, Matopos; MOZAMBIQUE: Maputo Elephant.

Black rhinoceros
Diceros bicornis
Swartrenoster

47

The tandem horns of the black rhino are more equal in size than those of the white rhino. The maximum length of the fore horn is 105 cm. It is not as large as that of the white rhino, with the maximum weight of the male about 850 kg and the female, 880 kg. The black rhino is the smaller of the two. Its actual colour is dark grey, much darker than the colour of the white rhino. See the text on the white rhino for further comparisons between the two species.

Black rhino are far more aggressive and bad-tempered than white rhino. The males of both species will do battle with competitors for the females, but battles between males of the black rhino are, in particular, very savage affairs. They are very territorial and, therefore, very subject to poaching.

As they are browsers, the black rhinos have prehensile hook-shaped upper lips to enable them to easily strip the leaves of trees and shrubs. They

BLACK RHINOCEROS

Gestation period: ± 455 days	
Young: one	
Mass: 850 kg.	
Shoulder height: 160 cm.	
Horns: ♂ length: max., 120 cm., aver. 65 cm. ♀ length: max., 60 cm., aver. 38 cm.	
Life expectancy: 40 years	

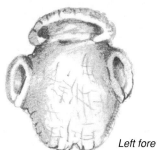

Left fore

¹⁄₆ actual size

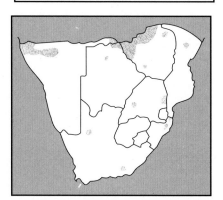

Left hind

prefer well-developed woodland or thickets for both food and resting needs and are more dependent on water than white rhinos. They are very fond of a mud wallow.

Enemies are rare. Lion and packs of wild dog may dare to attack what may appear to be a weakened animal. Female elephants show no fear and will, in temper, attack a black rhino and kill it. A single calf is produced. When walking through the bush the calf of the black rhino usually follows after its mother, while the white rhino calf usually precedes its mother.

Food: The staple food is leaves, twigs and soft branches and it will push over taller trees to get to the food. The prehensile upper lip is used to guide the shoots of plants to be bitten off by the pre-molars and then ground up between the massive molars. A large variety of shrub and tree species are browsed. In dry times some grass may be eaten. It is a selective feeder, selecting some plants and rejecting others. Black rhinos are particularly vulnerable to severe drought because of their sedentary nature.

Very rare and localised

Distribution: SOUTH AFRICA: *Transvaal*: Kruger Park, Londolozi, Messina, Nyala Ranch, Ohrigstad Dam, Percy Fyfe, Pilanesberg; *O.F.S.*: Maria Maroka; *Natal*: Hluhluwe, Itala, Oribi Gorge, St Lucia, Umfolozi, Weenen; *Cape*: Addo Elephant, Andries Vosloo, Aughrabies, Mkambati, Mountain Zebra, Oviston, Robberg, Vaalbos; SWAZILAND: Pongola.

NAMIBIA: Etosha, Naukluft, Skeleton Coast; BOTSWANA: Chobe; ZIMBABWE: Chete, Chewore, Chizarira, Gonarhezhou, Hwange, Malapati, Matopos, Nyanga; MOZAMBIQUE: Gorongosa

✓ ZEBRA

There are three species of zebra in the sub-region: Burchell's zebra, Cape Mountain zebra and Hartmann's Mountain Zebra. The latter two are relatively rare, being found in a restricted area, whereas Burchell's zebra is a widespread species, found throughout the central areas of Africa, from Ethiopia in the north to Zululand in the south. The distinctive stripes of the animals have a twofold purpose: the first being to camouflage the animals in bushy terrain, the second, to identify the mother to its young, as the distinct pattern of the stripes is exclusive to each individual animal. It will be seen that, immediately after birth, the mother will actively shield the foal from seeing any other animal for several hours, to give it time to imprint her image on its senses. If this is not done, and the foal imprints the image of another animal on its senses, it will follow that animal and not survive. This shielding process is sometimes very difficult when birth has occurred in the midst of a large herd.

It is argued that the difference between the two sub-species, the Cape mountain zebra and the Hartmann's mountain zebra, is insufficient for their separation and that they should comprise a single species.the Cape mountain zebra is smaller, some width difference is evidenced in the larger stripes on the rumps, and there is a difference in their ranges. There seems to be little valid reason for having a separate sub-species based on these minor differences and, despite the geographic inappropriateness of the name (as the Cape mountain zebra is the earliest taxa), some believe that the Cape Mountain zebra should be the valid name for both groups of animals. The Burchell's zebra lacks the dewlap found on the mountain zebras.

Burchell's zebra

Equus burchelli

Bontsebra *or* **Bontkwagga**

48

Several pattern features distinguish the Burchell's zebra from the other zebras, the occurrence of 'shadow' stripes between the heavy broad stripes on the hindquarters, the absence of the typical 'grid-iron' pattern on the top of the hindquarters and the lack of a dewlap. The patterns on the animals vary considerably and the shadow stripes may be relatively heavy or even, rarely, absent altogether. The males are recognised by their necks being thicker than those of the females.

Burchell's zebra are diurnal animals favouring open woodland and savannah, but avoiding desert and forest. They are very dependent upon readily available water and cannot utilise even optimum grazing conditions if water is not available. They are often found in close association with blue wildebeest. It has been shown that their main predator, the lion, has a preference for wildebeest and will take the wildebeest from a mixed herd, an association of distinct advantage for the zebra. They are gregarious animals, existing in small family groups of rarely more than nine animals, comprising a stallion, with one or more mares and their foals. Surplus males are ejected from the herd and form bachelor groups. Their vocalisation is a warning double 'ee-aa' or 'kwa-ha', or a loud snort. A long snort indicates contentment, fighting males voice short squeals and foals utter long squeals if afraid.

Defence is strong and takes the form of kicking and biting. Foals are sometimes kicked to death by a stallion. They will stoutly defend the herd, ganging up on a predator. The zebras main enemies are lion and they are also preyed upon by spotted hyaena and hunting dogs. The foals are food for leopards, and cheetah.

The Hartmann's zebra is preyed upon by lions in the limited area where their ranges overlap. The foals are vulnerable to smaller predators, such as

Left fore

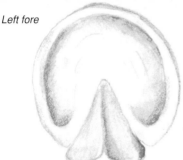

¹/₃ actual size

Left hind

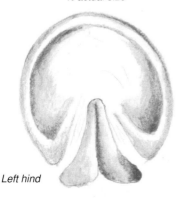

BURCHELL'S ZEBRA

Gestation period: ± 360 days

Young: one, rarely two

Mass: 320 kg.

Shoulder height: 135 cm.

Life expectancy: 40 years in captivity, usually 20 in the wild

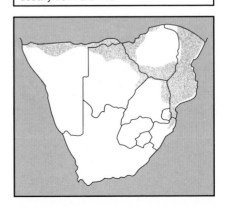

CAPE MOUNTAIN ZEBRA

Gestation period: ± 360 days

Young: one, rarely two

Mass: 250 kg.

Shoulder height: 125 cm.

Life expectancy: 20 years in the wild

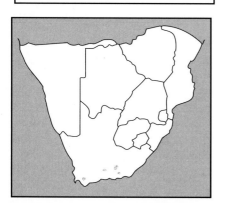

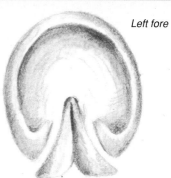

Left fore

½ actual size

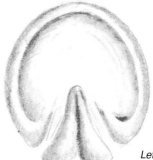

Left hind

Abundant and
widespread

leopard and caracal. They produce one, rarely two, active young.

Food: They are predominantly grazers but will occasionally browse. They also eat mineralised soils and the foals will eat the droppings of adults for the intestinal florae and bacilli. They will on occasion also drink saline water.

Distribution: SOUTH AFRICA: *Transvaal*: Ben Alberts, Ben Lavin, Blyde River Canyon, Borokalano, Doorndraai Dam, Hans Merensky, Hans Strydom Dam, Klaserie, Kruger Park, Langjan, Lapalala, Londolozi, Loskop Dam, Mala Mala, Manyeleti, Nylsvley, Ohrigstad Dam, Percy Fyfe, Pilanesberg, Roodeplaat Dam, Rustenburg, Sabi-Sabi, Sabi-Sand, S A Lombard, Timbavati, Umbabat/Motswari; *O.F.S.*: Bloemhof Dam, Erfenis Dam, Golden Gate, Maria Maroka, Soetdoring, Tussen-die-Riviere, Willem Pretorius; *Natal*: Hluhluwe, Kenneth Stainbank, Mkuzi, Ndumu, Phinda, St Lucia, Umfolozi, Weenen; *Cape*: Botsalano, Mkambati, Oviston, Rolfontein, Sandveld, Vaalbos.

SWAZILAND: Pongola; NAMIBIA: Eastern & Western Caprivi, Etosha, Kaudom, Mahonga; BOTSWANA: Chobe, Makgadikgadi, Mashatu, Moremi, Nxai Pan; ZIMBABWE: Chete, Chewore, Chizarira, Gonarhezhou, Hwange, Malapati, Mana Pools, Matopos, Matusadona; MOZAMBIQUE: Gorongosa, Maputa Elephant.

Cape mountain zebra
Equus zebra zebra
Kaapse bergsebra

49

This animal is dealt with under the next animal, the Hartmann's mountain zebra.

Hartmann's mountain zebra
Equus zebra hartmannae
Hartmann se bergsebra

50

Both animals are similar, the Cape mountain zebra is slightly smaller (maximum mass = ± 260kg) than the Hartmann's mountain zebra (maximum mass = ± 330kg). They are both gregarious, diurnal animals preferring mountainous areas. The Hartmann's also makes wide use of the sand flats. They are most active during early morning and late afternoon. The Cape mountain zebra, unlike the Hartmann's mountain zebra, makes no attempt to seek shade in the hottest times of the day, but this is probably due to the extremes of temperature in the Hartmann's range. Vocalisation of both is

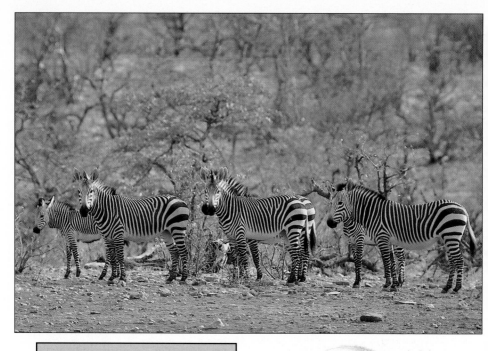

HARTMANN'S MOUNTAIN ZEBRA

Gestation period: ± 360 days

Young: one, rarely two

Mass: ♂ 290 kg, ♀ 275 kg.

Shoulder height: 150 cm.

Life expectancy: 20 years in the wild

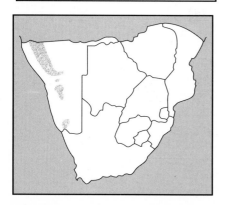

Left fore

½ actual size

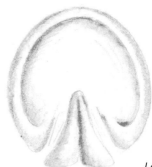
Left hind

similar: the alarm call being a short, sharp snort or 'kwa-ha'. See also the introductory paragraph on zebra and other details under Burchell's zebra.

Food: They are both grazers. The Cape mountain zebra is also known to browse. The presence of freely available water is essential. The foals also eat limited amounts of the faeces of the adult for the necessary intestinal micro-organism content. Because of its drier habitat, the Hartmann's will, if necessary, dig deep for water, providing water for a host of other animals.

Distribution: CAPE MOUNTAIN ZEBRA: SOUTH AFRICA: *O.F.S.*: Hendrik Verwoerd Dam; *Cape*: Bontebok, De Hoop, Gamkaberg, Karoo, Kommandodrift, Mountain Zebra, Robberg, Zuurberg.

HARTMANN'S MOUNTAIN ZEBRA: SOUTH AFRICA: *Cape*: Hester Malan; NAMIBIA: Daan Viljoen, Etosha, Hardap Dam, Naukluft, Skeleton Coast, Von Bach.

PIGS:

Two pig types are found in the sub-region. The diurnal warthogs are common inhabitants throughout the drier parts of the country, whereas the nocturnal bushpigs are fairly common but little-known inhabitants of dense bush and forest in the wetter regions. Warthogs are widely distributed throughout the entire continent and bushpigs occur in suitable habitat only up to the north-ern forested borders of the African continent. Bushpigs have one close relative, the giant forest hogs (*Hylochoerus meinertzhageni*), which are inhabi-tants of central Africa. The only other wild pigs of the continent are the wild boars (*Sus scrofa*) and these occur only in the north western parts of the con-tinent. The feral domestic pigs, also recorded as *Sus scrofa*, have been reported from the south western Cape. These are apparently descendents of domestic pigs released into the wild by the Department of Forestry in c.1942, for the control of the pine tree's pest, the pine tree emperor moth.

√ Warthog

Phacochoerus aethopicus

Vlakvark

51

These common wild pigs favour open ground, vleis, grasslands, waterholes and pans and they will also be seen in open woodland. Where the veld has been burned they will be seen grazing the newly-sprouted grass.

Two pairs of prominent wartlike excrescences on the face of the male and one pair on the face of the female give them their name. The maximum weight of the adult boar rarely exceeds 100 kg. Their tusks vary in size and some-times, particularly those of the female, attain a formidable length, curving high

WARTHOG

Gestation period: ± 165 days	
Young: two, rarely eight, usually two – four	
Mass: ♂ 80 kg, ♀ 55 kg.	
Shoulder height: ♂ 70 cm, ♀ 60 cm.	
Tusks: Canine teeth	
Life expectancy: 18 years	

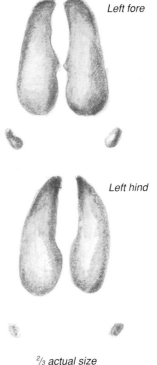

Left fore

Left hind

²/₃ *actual size*

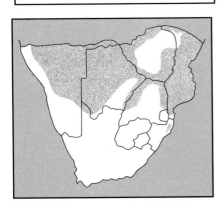

over the snout. Continual honing of the upper tusks against the bottom tusks keep both sets razor sharp, which makes the warthog a dangerous animal.

They live most commonly in deserted antbear burrows which they modify to their requirements, digging with their hooves and shovelling the loose earth out with their shovel-like snouts. The piglets enter the hole head-first, while the adults enter backwards. In an emergency bolt to the burrow the reversal will be accomplished at the very last moment, usually in a cloud of dust.

Warthogs do not depend on water, but drink copiously if it is available. Mud wallowing is a favourite pass-time.

The family sounder - or group - usually comprises the male, the female and piglets. After some time the male deserts the group but the bond between the female and piglets lasts longer, even up to three years. Should the female fall pregnant she may drive out the young. They depart to form sub-adult groups. The commonest sighting of a group is of the adults leading the off-spring, all with their tails held high, with the end tufts like little tattered flags at the end of a flag pole. To maintain contact the adults grunt and the piglets utter a whistling squeak. When under attack by a predator they snarl and snort.

Enemies are principally lion and leopard. Cheetah sometimes take the young. Litters are born in burrows which are sometimes grass-lined. Between one to eight, commonly three, piglets are produced. They will graze in about one week, are weaned at about nine weeks but continue suckling until about five months, remaining with their mothers until about one year old.

Food: The warthog is adept at digging with its hard shovel-shaped snout, which is a most effective digging tool. The animal kneels down and roots for tubers and rhizomes as deep as 15 cm. Its prime fare is the grasses and also the new grass sprouts after a burn. Berries and stripped-off tree bark are also eaten. The fallen fruit of the Marula Tree (*Sclerocarya caffra*) is a favourite food where it occurs. Not typical fare are sometimes snakes, litters of rats and carrion.

Common to abundant

Distribution: SOUTH AFRICA: *Transvaal*: Ben Alberts, Ben Lavin, Borokalano, Doorndraai Dam, Hans Merensky, Hans Strydom Dam, Klaserie, Kruger Park, Langjan, Lapalala, Londolozi, Loskop Dam, Mala Mala, Manyeleti, Messina, Nyala Ranch, Nylsvley, Pilanesberg, Sabi-Sabi, Sabi-Sand, Timbavati, Umbabat/ Motswari; *Natal*: False Bay, Hluhluwe, Itala, Mkuzi, Ndumu, Phinda, St Lucia, Umfolozi; *Cape*: Andries Vosloo, Botsalano, Kalahari Gemsbok, Rolfontein, Vaalbos.

NAMIBIA: Daan Viljoen, Eastern & Western Caprivi, Etosha, Hardap Dam, Kaudom, Mahonga, Naukluft, Skeleton Coast, Von Bach, Waterberg Plateau; BOTSWANA: Central Kalahari, Chobe, Khutse, Makgadikgadi, Mashatu, Moremi, Nxai Pan; ZIMBABWE: Chete, Chewore, Chizarira, Gonarhezhou, Hwange, Malapati, Mana Pools, Matopos, Matusadona; MOZAMBIQUE: Gorongosa.

BUSHPIG

Gestation period: ± 125 days	
Young: three, rarely eight, usually three – six	
Mass: 60 kg.	
Shoulder height: 65 cm.	
Life expectancy: 12 – 15 years	

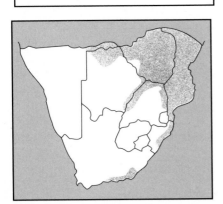

Left fore

Left hind

²/₃ *actual size*

Bushpig
Potamochoerus porcus
Bosvark

52

The bushpigs are also known as red river hogs in their northern range. Little-known, by virtue of their secretive and nocturnal habits, bushpigs are denizens of forest, riparian undercover, thick bush, reedbeds or tall thick grass. Proximity to water is essential. They will operate diurnally as well where they are not harassed. These large hairy pigs, which can weigh up to 80 kg, are gregarious, forming sounders of six to twelve animals, with a dominant boar, a sow and piglets. They aggressively defend their feeding ground and will vigorously and actively drive off intruding dominant boars. Encounters, however, are rarely serious. Like warthogs, they enjoy a good mud-wallow, probably as a defense against insect bites and as a temperature control method. They are aggressive and dangerous and will, rather than retreat, move forward and are more than able to inflict serious wounds with their sharp tusks.

Their principal predators are leopard and lion. Litters comprise three to eight, usually three to six piglets, born in the cover of thick bush, where they will make a nest lined with grass.

Food: They are omnivorous, eating grass, plants, leaves, fungi, small birds, young of small mammals, trapped animals and carrion, and are eager for salt licks.

Distribution: SOUTH AFRICA: *Transvaal*: Ben Alberts, Borokalano, Doorndraai Dam, Hans Strydom Dam, Klaserie, Kruger Park, Lapalala, Mala Mala, Manyeleti, Messina, Nyala Ranch, Nylsvley, Ohrigstad Dam, Pilanesberg, Sabi-Sabi, Sabi-Sand, Timbavati, Umbabat/Motswari; *Natal*: False Bay, Hluhluwe, Mkuzi, Ndumu, Phinda, St Lucia, Umfolozi; *Cape*: Addo Elephant, Andries Vosloo, Gamkapoort, Goukamma, Keurboom, Mountain Zebra, Thomas Baines, Tsitsikamma Coastal, Tsitsikamma Forest, Zuurberg.

NAMIBIA: Eastern & Western Caprivi; BOTSWANA: Chobe, Mashatu, Moremi; ZIMBABWE: Chete, Chewore, Chizarira, Gonarhezhou, Hwange, Malapati, Mana Pools, Matopos, Matusadona, Nyanga; MOZAMBIQUE: Gorongosa, Maputo Elephant.

Fairly common in a restricted area

✓ Hippopotamus
Hippopotamus amphibius
Seekoei

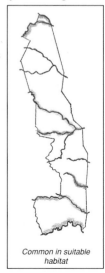

53

These semi-aquatic animals spend much of the day floating in their watery habitat, or lazing on mud banks. They favour permanent water with a sandy bottom, deep enough to submerge comfortably. Because of their bulk a fairly gentle sloping bank is needed to allow easy movement from the water. Rivers, dams and lakes are equally acceptable but hippos have a preference for water offering permanent pools in which they remain, sometimes for years. They keep rivers and estuaries clean from reeds and silt build-up and their disappearance from many southern African rivers has been detrimental to the ecology.

The red colouring of the hide is an oily, viscous lubricant secreted as a protection from the sun. For, unlike land mammals, they do not usually lie under trees. They also float immobile in the water with drying backs and heads exposed to the harsh African sun. Despite this protective secretion they cannot remain too long in the sun as skin damage could occur.

Normal herds number up to 15 animals, sometimes more, which comprise a dominant bull, females, sub-adults and young. Solitary bulls are also encountered. The dominant male is very territorial, savagely defending his herd from any interloper and marking his territory by defecating in the water, on bushes and rocks with the characteristic side-ways flicking of the tail. This territorial behaviour diminishes or even disappears at the feeding grounds.

At night the animals leave the water and head for their grazing grounds, which can be as much as 30 km away, making well-defined paths which are like twin tracks, made by the feet on either side of the wide animal. If surprised while returning to the water, they can be extremely dangerous to anyone crossing their path. They are probably responsible for the deaths of more humans in Africa than any other wild animals. Hippos are often found walking along the bottom of deep water. Similar to their habit on dry land they often use the same path which can sometimes be clearly seen.

Adult hippos can remain under water for as long as six minutes, surfacing with the sound of a loud hissing blast of expelled air, which is audible for a long way. They are not afraid of entering the sea and are occasionally

Common in suitable habitat

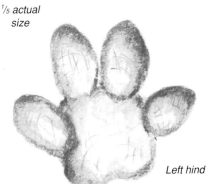

Left fore

$^1/_5$ actual
size

HIPPOPOTAMUS

Gestation period: ± 250 days	
Young: one, rarely two	
Mass: ♂ 1 500 kg, ♀ 1 400 kg.	
Shoulder height: ♂ 150 cm, ♀ 140 cm.	
Life expectancy: 40 – 45 years, up to 50 years in zoos	

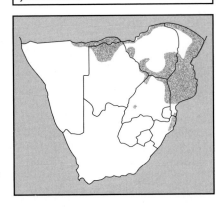

Left hind

encountered beyond the breakers on the northern Natal coast. Their voice is a deep roaring grunt, followed by five shorter grunts in quick succession. This occurs most frequently around sunset.

The female leaves the open water to give birth to a single calf, or rarely two, in a secluded place in reedbeds. The calf is able to swim within a few minutes of birth and is carefully guarded by the mother, as it is a favourite fare of crocodiles.

Food: Hippos are prodigious feeders; their main food is grass, which they crop with the horny edges of their lips, almost as closely as a lawnmower. They are notorious crop-raiders.

Distribution: SOUTH AFRICA: *Transvaal*: Blyde River Canyon, Hans Merensky, Hans Strydom Dam, Klaserie, Kruger Park, Lapalala, Londolozi, Mala Mala, Manyeleti, Pilanesberg, Sabi-Sabi, Sabi-Sand, Umbabat/Motswari; *Natal*: Hluhluwe, Mkuzi, Ndumu, St Lucia, Phinda.

SWAZILAND: Pongola; NAMIBIA: Eastern & Western Caprivi, Mahonga; BOTSWANA: Chobe, Mashatu, Moremi; ZIMBABWE: Chete, Chewore, Gonarhezhou, Hwange, Mana Pools, Matopos, Matusadona; MOZAMBIQUE: Gorongosa, Maputo Elephant.

GIRAFFE

The family Giraffidae is represented by the very rare Okapi (*Okapia johnstoni*) which is a denizen of the Ituri forests of N.E. Zaïre and the common giraffe. There are several sub-species of the giraffe but only two sub-species occur in the subregion: one from south-eastern Zimbabwe, Transvaal and Mozambique and the other from western Zimbabwe, Botswana and Namibia. Their division throughout Africa into sub-species is based only upon the patterns of their marking, the criteria being the shape of the patches and the width of the dividing light areas between the dark patches.

√ Giraffe

Giraffa camelopardalis

Kameelperd

54

This is the tallest animal on earth, growing up to about 5 metres. The tallest recorded, an exceptional animal from Kenya, measured nearly six metres. The 'horns' or sub-conical ossicones are topped with black hair and look like knobs. There is sometimes a smaller 'horn' or knob, between the two 'horns'. They have stiff, bristle-like manes, extending from the top of the head between the horns to the top of the shoulders. The extraordinary neck has seven elongated vertebrae, the same number as has man. Special valves in the carotid artery and jugular vein prevent flooding or evacuation of blood from the skull when the head is either lowered or raised.

Right fore

Right hind

¹/₃ actual size

GIRAFFE	
Gestation period: ± 440 days	
Young: one, rarely two	
Mass: ♂ 1 200 kg, ♀ 850 kg.	
Shoulder height: ♂ 330 cm, ♀ 280 cm.	
Life expectancy: 28 years	

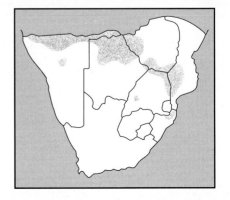

Their preferred habitat is bushy or open scrubby plains with *acacia* trees, which is their favoured food. They are not generally associated with open plains. They will drink if water is available but this is not essential as they appear to be able to subsist on water from their food plants.

Giraffe are predominantly diurnal, but will also move and feed after dark. They rest in the hottest part of the day, sometimes with the head resting in the fork of a tree.

Social structure is not strong and bulls wander from one herd to another and leadership appears to be loose, with no apparent established hierarchy. Although they are docile, they will defend themselves stoutly against their main predator, the lion. They have been known to kill a lion by a sharp forward chop of their forelegs. Smaller predators than lion will try and take their young.

The males spar in the mating season with characteristic swinging of their necks against each other, butting with the horns and using the head as a club. This is the probable reason for the male's larger head and horns. These fights are rarely serious and little damage is done. One calf is born, rarely twins.

Food: Almost exclusively browsers, they eat a wide variety of leaves and twigs. Acacias are preferred and have proved to have a high degree of protein. They will eat newly sprouted grass and will eagerly eat mineralised soil or even gnaw on bones for the mineral content.

Distribution: SOUTH AFRICA: *Transvaal*: Ben Alberts, Ben Lavin, Borokalano, Doorndraai Dam, Hans Merensky, Klaserie, Kruger Park, Langjan, Lapalala, Londolozi, Loskop Dam, Mala Mala, Manyeleti, Messina, Nyala Ranch, Nylsvley, Pilanesberg, Rustenburg, Sabi-Sabi, Sabi-Sand, Timbavati, Umbabat/Motswari; *O.F.S.*: Willem Pretorius; *Natal*: Hluhluwe, Itala, Kenneth Stainbank, Mkuzi, Phinda, Umfolozi, Weenen; *Cape*: Botsalano, Vaalbos.

NAMIBIA: Eastern & Western Caprivi, Etosha, Kaudom, Skeleton Coast, Waterberg Plateau; BOTSWANA: Central Kalahari, Chobe, Khutse, Makgadikgadi, Mashatu, Moremi, Nxai Pan; ZIMBABWE: Gonarhezhou, Hwange, Malapati, Matopos.

Common to very common, rarer northwards

WILDEBEEST:

Two wildebeest species are found in the sub-region. The most ubiquitous being the blue wildebeest, which has a large range, extending well into East Africa, whereas the black wildebeest is endemic to the southern and central parts of South Africa.

Black wildebeest

Connochaetes gnou

Swartwildebees

55

These animals once ranged in their hundreds of thousands across the central open karoid plains of South Africa. Persistent hunting and agricultural development has taken them almost to the brink of extinction. Conservation measures halted this slide, but even today they are rarely encountered outside of designated conservation areas. Also known as the white-tailed gnu ('gnu' being the Hottentot name derived from the sound of the animal's snort), these peculiar animals, which run with a characteristic rocking-horse motion, are bad-tempered and dangerous animals when cornered. Both sexes carry horns, with those of the female being shorter and less robust.

The social structure of these gregarious animals involves dominant territorial males, females and bachelor herds. This dominant male is usually only displaced when it is too weak to defend itself from the up-and-coming young male challenger of four or more years of age. Only these males take part in the rut, preventing younger males from participating. In the preamble to the rut they advertise their presence with loud bi-syllabic calls of 'ga-nu', which is accompanied with many territorial antics which include scent-marking.

When resting they do not always seek shade, but rest lying down with the rump towards the sun. They are diurnal and active in the cooler parts of the day and in hot weather before sunrise and after sunset. They are easily 'spooked' and will readily stampede at a perceived danger.

The major enemies in their areas are now extinct, with the exception of the black-backed jackal, which will bring down a calf. Only one calf is produced.

Food: They are predominantly grazers but will, in the winter months browse the karoid bushes. They are dependent on water and will drink twice daily.

Distribution: SOUTH AFRICA: *Transvaal*: Barberspan, S A Lombard, Suikerbosrand; *O.F.S.*: Bloemhof Dam, Erfenis Dam, Golden Gate, Hendrik Verwoerd Dam, Maria Maroka, Soetdoring, Tussen-die-Riviere, Willem Pretorius; *Natal*: Giants Castle, Kamberg, Royal Natal; *Cape*: Botsalano, Karoo, Kommandodrift, Mountain Zebra, Oviston, Rolfontein, Salmon's Dam, Thomas Baines, Vaalbos.

BLACK WILDEBEEST

Gestation period: ± 250 days	
Young: one	
Mass: ♂ 180 kg, ♀ 145 kg.	
Shoulder height: ♂ 120 cm, ♀ 110 cm.	
Horns: 75 cm.	
Life expectancy: 19 years	

Left fore

½ actual size

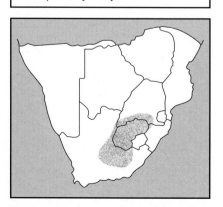

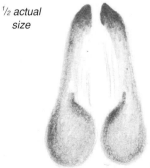

Left hind

Left fore

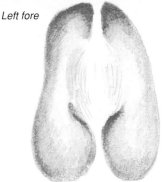

$^1/_2$ *actual size*

Left hind

BLUE WILDEBEEST

Gestation period: ± 250 days	
Young: one	
Mass: ♂ 250 kg, ♀ 180 kg.	
Shoulder height: ♂ 150 cm, ♀ 135 cm.	
Horns: 70 cm.	
Life expectancy: 18 years	

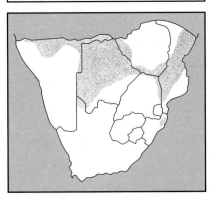

√ Blue wildebeest
Connochaetes taurinus
Blouwildebees

56

Although these animals have never approached extinction like the black wildebeest, the numbers are a far cry from the massive herds which roamed the plains of the early habitat, particularly East Africa. There are, however, still areas of fairly large herd aggregations. In this sub-region, Botswana still sees large herd movements. Their preferred habitat is open grassland, flood-plain grassland and bush savanna, but will also utilise light woodland. Water is an essential component of their habitat.

They are diurnal and are most active during the morning and late afternoon, resting in the heat of the day. On cooler days are active all day and also active on moonlit nights. The territorial male will indulge in a variety of territorial displays to suit the occasion. It will dissuade an interloper with a threat display, involving erect neck and forward directed head and a rocking-horse cantering motion forward, which is usually sufficient to send the other male off. Males will herd females with a lowered head, and streaming tail, grunting and lowing. Young females may stay in the herd for life but males are sent off to join bachelor groups. Both sexes carry horns with those of the female being less robust

Predators are lion, leopard, cheetah, hyaena, wild dog and for calves, also black-backed jackal. Great mortality through drowning and trampling has been recorded in the massive migrations. This pro-vides a feast for predators and scavengers, which follow the herds to pick out the weak and young. The wildebeest is a prey favoured by the lion above the zebra. The zebra, it is believed, senses this and associates with the wilde-beest herds for the safety the association provides.

Females in oestrus move restlessly from one territo-rial bull to another, mating with several. Copulation is usually at night. One precocial calf is born and must be able to move with the herd at a very early age if it is to escape the predators.

Food: They are grazers, eating usually only very short grass. Their spatulate shaped muzzle allows them to feed on the very short grass. They particularly favour newly-sprouted grass after a fire.

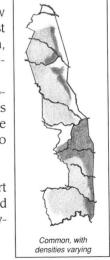

Common, with densities varying

Distribution: SOUTH AFRICA: *Transvaal*: Ben Alberts, Ben Lavin, Blyde River Canyon, Borokalano, Doorndraai Dam, Hans Merensky, Klaserie, Kruger Park, Lapalala, Londolozi, Loskop Dam, Mala Mala, Manyeleti, Nylsvley, Pilanesberg, Roodeplaat Dam, Sabi-Sabi, Sabi-Sand, Timbavati, Umbabat/Motswari; *O.F.S.*: Hendrik Verwoerd Dam, Tussen-die-Riviere; *Natal*: Hluhluwe, Mkuzi, Phinda, Umfolozi; *Cape*: Botsalano, Kalahari Gemsbok, Mkambati, Sandveld, Vaalbos; SWAZILAND: Pongola.

NAMIBIA: Daan Viljoen, Etosha, Kaudom, Mahonga, Waterberg Plateau; BOTSWANA: Central Kalahari, Chobe, Gemsbok, Khutse, Mabuasehube, Makgadikgadi, Moremi, Mashatu, Nxai Pan; ZIMBABWE: Gonarhezhou, Hwange, Matopos, Nyanga; MOZAMBIQUE: Gorongosa.

HARTEBEEST:

Two hartebeest species are found in the subregion. Lichtenstein's harte-beests (*Alcelaphus lichtensteinii*) was found in the western parts of the Transvaal but died out. Their habit of standing on an anthill to survey the countryside, thus being easily exposing to the hunter's gun, probably aided their demise. They have since been re-introduced into the Kruger Park, and a few private reserves, but are, however, still rare. The red hartebeest has a fairly wide distribution and was first recorded in the subregion in the south western Cape at the time of Van Riebeeck (c.1660).

Red hartebeest
Alcelaphus buselaphus
Rooihartbees

The elongated appearance of the head is even more exaggerated in this species than in Lichtenstein's Hartebeest, as the pedicle is long and the lower, smooth, unringed section of horn is also long, continuing in line with the face. The ridged section curves forward and then backwards and the smooth tip continues to a point. Both sexes carry horns with those of the female being less robust. The whitish rump, blackish upper haunch, and the inverted V-shaped blackish marking, extending to the knee on the upper foreleg, is characteristic.

In flight the rocking-horse motion is comically exaggerated by the up and down bobbing of the long, rather lugubrious face. Like *A. lichtensteinii*, they are intensely inquisitive and the herd will pause, even in their headlong swerving flight, to mill around and take stock of the situation.

These are gregarious animals, forming herds of usually 20, up to more than 300, animals in suitable habitat. The males are very territorial in habit and will viciously defend their territories against other males. In the absence of a dominant male, leadership may be temporarily assumed by an adult female.

Vocalisation and reproduction is similar to that of the tsessebe, as are their enemies.

RED HARTEBEEST

Gestation period: ± 240 days	
Young: one	
Mass: ♂ 150 kg, ♀ 120 kg.	
Shoulder height: 135 cm.	
Horns: 60 cm.	
Life expectancy: 19 years in captivity	

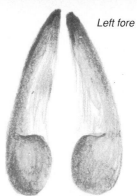

Left fore

¹/₂ *actual size*

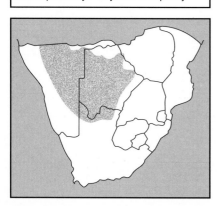

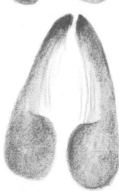

Left hind

Distribution: SOUTH AFRICA: *Transvaal*: Barberspan, Ben Alberts, Borokalano, Langjan, Lapalala, Messina, Nyala Ranch, Pilanesberg, Rustenburg, S A Lombard, Suikerbosrand; *O.F.S.*: Bloemhof Dam, Erfenis Dam, Hendrik Verwoerd Dam, Maria Maroka, Soetdoring, Tussen-die-Riviere, Willem Pretorius; *Natal*: Giants Castle, Kamberg, Royal Natal, Weenen; *Cape*: Addo Elephant, Andries Vosloo, Aughrabies, Botsalano, Kalahari Gemsbok, Karoo, Mkambati, Mountain Zebra, Oviston, Rolfontein, Sandveld, Vaalbos, Zuurberg.

NAMIBIA: Daan Viljoen, Etosha, Hardap Dam, Kaudom, Waterberg Plateau; BOTSWANA: Central Kalahari, Gemsbok, Khutse, Mabuasehube, Makgadikgadi; ZIMBABWE: Hwange.

BONTEBOK, BLESBOK AND TSESSEBE

Previously considered two separate species, the bontebok and blesbok have now been accorded only subspecies status. Nevertheless these two animals are distinctive in appearance and are disjunct in their range. The tsessebe is a larger animal, which has a black, not a white, blaze on its face and the limbs are wholly coloured.

✓Bontebok
Damaliscus dorcas dorcas
Bontebok

58

These are probably one of the most beautifully marked and attractive of the antelope. The deep purplish colour contrasting with the pure white and the rust-brown of the back, together with the white facial blaze, which extends unbroken from the top of the head to the rhinarium, sets these animals apart. Occasionally the white blaze is broken by a dark band between the eyes. Both sexes carry horns. In the middle 1800s they were approaching extinction, but imaginative conservation practise saw them back from the brink and they are now safe in the confines of reservations, in their limited range in the south western Cape. Their habitat is the macchia and renoster-bos areas of high winter rainfall.

They are diurnal, gregarious animals, with a territorial hierarchy of female and bachelor herds and territorial males which maintain a range or mosaic of territories, retained by a ritualistic display system rarely involving fighting. In the rut males endeavour to entice the females into their territories, and, by herding and ritualistic behaviour, to retain them. The female herd is dominated by an adult female which drives off any over-attentive young males and maintains dominance among her own with threat, clashing of horns and display. In the bachelor herd, the largest group, there is safe haven for young males, some yearling females and old bulls. There is no hierarchical dominance in this herd.

Virtually no predators of any importance threatens the remaining bontebok. One precocial calf is produced.

BONTEBOK

Gestation period: ± 240 days	
Young: one	
Mass: 60 kg.	
Shoulder height: 90 cm.	
Horns: 40 cm.	
Life expectancy: 15 years	

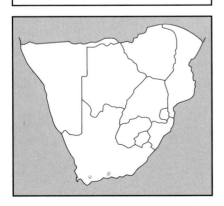

Left fore

Left hind

$^1/_2$ *actual size*

Left fore

¹/₂ actual size

BLESBOK

Gestation period: ± 240 days	
Young: one	
Mass: ♂ 70 kg, ♀ 60 kg.	
Shoulder height: 95 cm.	
Horns: 50 cm.	
Life expectancy: 15 years, 17 years in zoos	

Left hind

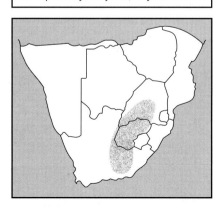

Food: They are almost exclusively grazers and the presence of free water is essential.

Distribution: *Cape*: Bontebok, Cape Point, De Hoop, Goukamma.

Blesbok
Damaliscus dorcas phillipsi
Blesbok

59

In earlier times there was probably a continuous range between the present-day bontebok and blesbok. This was interrupted and the two distinct sub-species evolved. In most respects they are similar. The blesbok is much more drab and the coat is uniformly brown with only the underparts being off-white and the inside of the ears white. The blaze is divided in two by a band between the eyes. This interruption is very occasionally absent. Both sexes carry horns.

In common with the bontebok is the curious characteristic behavioural trait of standing together with their heads orientated towards the sun and faces close to the ground, sometimes accompanied with violent head-shaking and stamping and running in a full circle to resume their vacated place.

During the colder seasons the groups aggregate into very large herds. All sexes are included, sometimes up to as many as 600 individuals. They differ from the bontebok, in that the social structure undergoes change through the seasons, whereas the structures of the bontebok remain static.

Reproduction and territorial behaviour is similar to that of the bontebok.

Food: They are almost exclusively grazers and will avidly enter a burnt area and eat the charcoal and ash of the fire, as well as the newly sprouted grass. Available water is essential.

Distribution: SOUTH AFRICA: *Transvaal*: Barberspan, Ben Alberts, Borokalano, Lapalala, Loskop Dam, Ohrigstad Dam, S A Lombard, Sterkspruit, Suikerbosrand; *O.F.S.*: Bloemhof Dam, Erfenis Dam, Golden Gate, Hendrik Verwoerd Dam, Maria Maroka, Soetdoring, Tussen-die-Riviere, Willem Pretorius; *Natal*: Giants Castle, Kamberg, Royal Natal; *Cape*: Amalinda, Botsalano, Kommandodrift, Mkambati, Mountain Zebra, Oviston, Rolfontein, Vaalbos, Zuurberg.

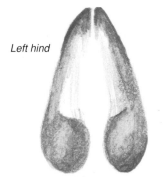

¹/₂ *actual size*

Left fore

Left hind

TSESSEBE
Gestation period: ± 235 days
Young: one
Mass: ♂ 140 kg, ♀ 120 kg.
Shoulder height: 120 cm.
Horns: 45 cm.
Life expectancy: 15 years

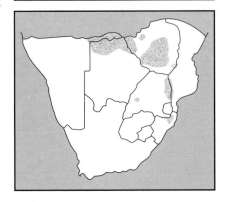

Tsessebe
Damaliscus lunatus
Tsessebe

60

The strange name is derived from the Tswana name, tshêsêbe. These antelope are larger and quite different in appearance to the other two animals of the genus. The horns are more splayed and there is a black rather than a white blaze on the face. The colour is a darkish brown with a metallic sheen; there is a large shoulder hump and the back slopes characteristically. Both sexes carry horns. They are very fleet of foot. Inquisitive by nature, they will run a short distance, stop and look back, even if extreme danger threatens. Although they appear to be ungainly they are able to run at speed for considerable distances. They will stand on anthills, with the head raised as a threatening gesture to rivals, and will fight on their knees with clashing horns.

Tsessebe are diurnal, gregarious animals, and will sometimes associate with zebra, wildebeest and ostriches, occasionally forming large herds of hundreds of animals. Unlike the bontebok the harems remain permanently with the territorial male, a disadvantage when the dominant male may become infertile. Their behaviour includes horning the ground from a kneeling position and both sexes will do so.

Fairly common in specific areas

Enemies include the large predators: lions, leopards, wild dog and spotted hyaena. The young are preyed upon by caracal, jackal, serval, python and large raptors. Their family hierarchy consists of up to twelve animals with their calves. Only one is produced at a time.

Food: They eat grass and herbage almost exclusively, rarely leaves.

Distribution: SOUTH AFRICA: *Transvaal*: Borokalano, Doorndraai Dam, Kruger Park, Lapalala, Mala Mala, Messina, Nyala Ranch, Nylsvley, Percy Fyfe, Pilanesberg, Umbabat/Motswari; *Natal*: Itala; *Cape*: Botsalano.

NAMIBIA: Eastern & Western Caprivi, Kaudom, Mahonga, Waterberg Plateau; BOTSWANA: Chobe, Moremi; ZIMBABWE: Chizarira, Hwange, Matopos.

DUIKER

Two genera comprise the three species of this sub-region's duikers, which are small to medium antelope with slender legs and heads and rounded backs. Their horns lie more or less in line with the head, and the eyes are relatively large, with preorbital glands which, if pressed, ooze a fluid with which territories are marked. They favour bush cover.

√ Common duiker

Sylvicapra grimmia

Gewone duiker

61

Also known as the grey or crowned duiker, these small antelope vary considerably in colour, from greyish-buff to reddish-yellow across their range. Underparts are whitish. Males have a tuft of long black or brown hair between the horns. There is a broad dark band from the horns down to the nostrils, but sometimes only confined to the lower part of the face. The front of the lower forelegs is black. Only males have horns, maximum length about 18 cm, but very occasionally the females have short stunted horns.

They are solitary, mainly diurnal animals, active usually in the early mornings and late afternoons, with activity extending late into the night, especially on clear moonlit nights. They are habitually secretive and, if disturbed, will steal away with head lowered and tail up, or will leap away at the last moment, stopping a short distance away to look back. Will scream loudly and fight furiously if captured, using both the back legs and sharp horns with good effect. Normally a quiet species, they will occasionally snort nasally. The young will bleat loudly if afraid.

Enemies are many. They are taken by all the larger predators, serval, wildcats, civets, larger genets, hunting dog, jackal, hyaena, baboons, honey badger, eagles, large owls, crocodiles, monitor lizards and pythons.

A single calf is produced, born in the depths of thick vegetation. After cleaning and suckling it will be left well hidden and returned to from time to time for suckling. Its development to independence and adulthood is very rapid.

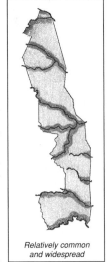

Relatively common and widespread

Food: Almost exclusively browsers, will rarely eat grass. They are remarkably omnivorous, eating berries and fruit, carrion, flesh, termites, ants, lizards and snakes, small

Right fore

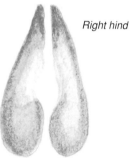

Right hind

Actual size

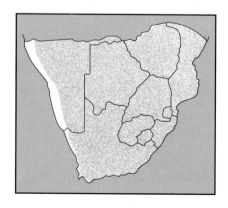

COMMON DUIKER	
Gestation period: ± 250 days	
Young: one	
Mass: ♂ 18 kg, ♀ 20 kg.	
Shoulder height: ♂ 50 cm, ♀ 52 cm.	
Horns: 16 cm.	
Life expectancy: 11 years	

ground birds including the young of guineafowl. They are delicate eaters and can be problem animals in that they nip off the tenderest twigs and shoots from ornamental shrubbery, agricultural crops and young plantation trees. Will rarely drink, relying on their diet for water.

Distribution: SOUTH AFRICA: *Transvaal*: Ben Alberts, Ben Lavin, Borokalano, Doorndraai Dam, Hans Merensky, Hans Strydom Dam, Klaserie, Kruger Park, Langjan, Lapalala, Londolozi, Loskop Dam, Mala Mala, Manyeleti, Messina, Nyala Ranch, Nylsvley, Ohrigstad Dam, Percy Fyfe, Pilanesberg, Roodeplaat Dam, Rustenburg, Sabi-Sabi, Sabi-Sand, S A Lombard, Sterkspruit, Suikerbosrand, Timbavati, Umbabat/Motswari; *O.F.S.*: Erfenis Dam, Hendrik Verwoerd Dam, Soetdoring, Tussen-die-Riviere, Willem Pretorius; *Natal*: False Bay, Giants Castle, Hluhluwe, Kamberg, Kenneth Stainbank, Loteni, Mkuzi, Ndumu, Oribi Gorge, Phinda, Royal Natal, St Lucia, Umfolozi, Weenen; *Cape*: Addo Elephant, Amalinda, Andries Vosloo, Aughrabies, Bontebok, Botsalano, De Hoop, Gamkaberg, Gamkapoort, Hester Malan, Kalahari Gemsbok, Karoo, Kommandodrift, Langebaan, Mkambati, Mountain Zebra, Oviston, Rocher Pan, Rolfontein, Sandveld, Thomas Baines, Vaalbos, Zuurberg.

SWAZILAND: Pongola; NAMIBIA: Daan Viljoen, Eastern & Western Caprivi, Etosha, Hardap Dam, Kaudom, Mahonga, Skeleton Coast, Waterberg Plateau; BOTSWANA: Central Kalahari, Chobe, Gemsbok, Khutse, Mabuasehube, Makgadikgadi, Mashatu, Moremi, Nxai Pan; ZIMBABWE: Chete, Chewore, Chizarira, Gonarhezhou, Hwange, Malapati, Matopos, Mana Pools, Matusadona, Nyanga; MOZAMBIQUE: Gorongosa, Maputo Elephant.

Red duiker
Cephalophus natalensis
Rooiduiker

62

Smaller than the common duiker and larger than the blue duiker, the main distinguishing features are their chestnut-red colour (Mozambique specimens are more orange) and the crest of long, partly chestnut and partly black, bushy hair on the top of the head. The outside edges of the ears are fringed with black hair. Both sexes have a pair of short, straight horns, which lie in the line of the face. The female's horns are weaker.

These rarely seen antelope are usually solitary but will, however, form loose associations. They are shy, secretive and difficult to spot in their preferred habitat of forest and dense thickets, favouring riverine forest, ravines, forest-decked mountain slopes and dense coastal bush. If encountered they almost immediately bound away. Their voice is a loud 'tschie-tschie'.

Enemies are similar to the other duikers. Only one all black young is born. Twins are rarely produced.

Very rare and localised

Food: They are browsers, but some grass is eaten, particularly the fresh sprouts of burnt grass. They eat the fallen fruit of the forest fig and other trees knocked off by

RED DUIKER

Gestation period: unknown	
Young: one, rarely two	
Mass: 14 kg.	
Shoulder height: 43 cm.	
Horns: 9 cm.	
Life expectancy: 12 years	

Left fore

Actual size

Left hind

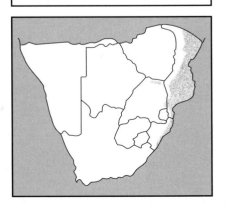

the green pigeons, baboons, vervet and samango monkeys. They drink water regularly and are dependent upon its supply.

Distribution: SOUTH AFRICA: *Transvaal*: Kruger Park, Sterkspruit; *Natal*: False Bay, Hluhluwe, Kenneth Stainbank, Mkuzi, Ndumu, Phinda, St Lucia, Umfolozi; *Cape*: Zuurberg.
SWAZILAND: Pongola; MOZAMBIQUE: Gorongosa, Maputo Elephant.

Blue duiker
Cephalophus monticola
Blouduiker

Also known in central Africa as Maxwell's duiker, they are the smallest antelope of the sub-region, measuring a bare 30 cm to the shoulder. Their colour is a dark smoky brown with a distinct bluish sheen. Both sexes have tiny horns, 30-35 mm long, the longest measured was about 57 mm, sometimes so small that they can be obscured by the slightly longer hair on the top of the head. The muzzle is slightly trunk-like and the eyes are placed slightly more forward than most small antelope. The preorbital glands are slightly protuberant.

Usually solitary, they are secretive, silent and difficult to spot. Their vocalisation, if they are caught, is a loud cat-like miaouw. They are confined to forest, dense thickets and dense bush, creating well-marked forest paths between their lying-up, feeding and drinking places. Extremely shy and timid they come out into the open with great reluctance and care, running back rapidly at the least hint of danger.

Enemies, which include indigenous people, who trap along their forest paths, are similar to the common duiker.

Little is known of their reproduction habits except that they pair briefly and bear one lamb.

Food: Similar eating habits as the red duiker.

Distribution: SOUTH AFRICA: *Natal*: Hluhluwe, Kenneth Stainbank, Oribi Gorge, St Lucia; *Cape*: Amalinda, Andries Vosloo, Goukamma, Keurboom, Thomas Baines, Tsitsikamma Coastal, Tsitsikamma Forest, Zuurberg.
ZIMBABWE: Nyanga; MOZAMBIQUE: Gorongosa

BLUE DUIKER

Gestation period: ± 120 days	
Young: one, rarely two	
Mass: ♂ 4,5 kg, ♀ 5,5 kg.	
Shoulder height: 30 cm.	
Horns: 9 cm.	
Life expectancy: 7 years	

Left fore

Actual size

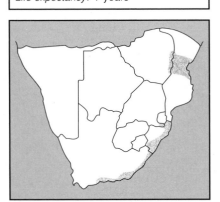

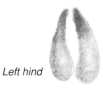

Left hind

Springbok

Antidorcas marsupialis

Springbok

64

Probably the only true gazelle found in the subregion, with some maintaining that the impala is also a gazelle. These beautiful and graceful antelopes are inhabitants of the more arid western parts of the country. In early days they roamed free in their millions, covering the landscape as they migrated from place to place and before the turn of the century an eye-witness account recorded that the 'trekbokken' (migrating buck) covered the ground like a fall of snow, moving in a mass a hundred miles long by fifteen miles wide. Such an awesome sight must have more than rivalled the vast herds of wildebeest migrating in East Africa. They have been known to trek west in Namaqualand and, when the sea was reached, drink thirstily, perishing as a result in their many thousands. In South Africa they are now found confined only to reserves and farms.

They are unmistakable animals; both males and females carry horns, although those of the females are smaller and thinner. They are gregarious and form small herds. When migration is necessary, to find green grazing, they may aggregate in large herds in excess of a thousand animals and follow the rain patterns. They are loosely territorial and a male may retain a female herd, but will not force them to remain if they wish to leave. They also form large bachelor groups.

The movement of the springbok is that of grace and beauty. Normally they move slowly but will break out into a fast trot. They will trot with a springy, proud, high step, accompanied by head shaking. They can gallop at speeds of in excess of 80 km per hour, which is accomplished with ears laid back. Stotting is not unique to the springbok, being also practised by oribis. It is, however, most dramatic and accomplished in the springbok which, in stress or while being pursued, will bounce repeatedly, high in the air, stiff-legged, with all feet meeting the ground together and with arched back. The dorsal plume of white hair, which is normally covered by a sheath of brown hair, is erected like a fan and shown to perfection in this bout of spectacular display.

They associate loosely with other antelope, such as black wildebeest, hartebeest, blesbok, gemsbok and also ostriches.

Usually silent, they will sometimes contact with a grunt-like bellow. The alarm call is a high-pitched whistling snort. Their enemies are cheetah, lion, leopard, and for the fawns, caracal, badger, African wild cat, black-backed jackals and eagles. They produce one fawn, and rarely twins, which is precocial.

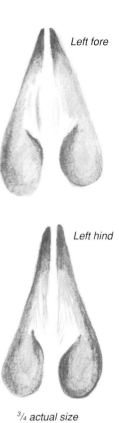

Left fore

Left hind

$^3/_4$ *actual size*

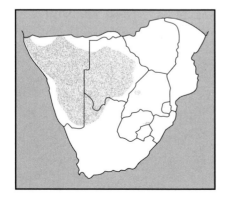

SPRINGBOK

Gestation period: ± 180 days

Young: one

Mass: ♂ 40 kg, ♀ 35 kg.

Shoulder height: 75 cm.

Horns: 45 cm.

Life expectancy: 10 years

Food: They are both grazers and browsers, eating the karoid bushes, the leaves and shoots of trees and grass.

Distribution: SOUTH AFRICA: *Transvaal*: Barberspan, Pilanesberg, Rustenburg, S A Lombard, Suikerbosrand; *O.F.S.*: Bloemhof Dam, Erfenis Dam, Golden Gate, Hendrik Verwoerd Dam, Maria Maroka, Soetdoring, Tussen-die-Riviere, Willem Pretorius; *Cape*: Andries Vosloo, Aughrabies, Bontebok, Botsalano, De Hoop, Hester Malan, Kalahari Gemsbok, Karoo, Kommandodrift, Mkambati, Mountain Zebra, Oviston, Rocher Pan, Rolfontein, Salmon's Dam, Sandveld, Vaalbos.

NAMIBIA: Daan Viljoen, Etosha, Hardap Dam, Naukluft, Skeleton Coast; BOTSWANA: Central Kalahari, Gemsbok, Khutse, Mabuasehube, Makgadikgadi, Nxai Pan

Klipspringer

Oreotragus oreotragus

Klipspringer

65

Klipspringers are small antelope, ideally suited to their rocky habitat. Their hair, which rustles when stroked, is hollow, flattened, springy, spiny, adhering loosely to the skin and is easily shed. Its springiness prevents damage to the animal from hard bumps against rocks and provides insulation against heat, cold and loss of body heat. The animal's colour depends on the penultimate band of colour, or the colour of the tip of the hair. It ranges from golden yellow to blackish-grey. The colour changes along the hair shaft imparting a speckled effect to the coat. They move on the tips of their unique hooves, which are of a consistency of very hard rubber. In this region only males have horns, but in parts of Tanzania and further north, some females carry weak thinner horns. They have clearly seen, rounded preorbital glands immediately in front of the eyes.

As the name suggests, they make their home in rocky areas; they use anything from rocky boulder-strewn riverbeds, rocky outcrops on plains, to rocky hills and kranzes, with thick bush for concealment as an important habitat component. They are very fast and agile, leaping and bouncing up impossible rock-faces from boulder to boulder, easily eluding any pursuer. They are usually encountered standing motionless in their characteristic pose against the skyline, at the very top of their rocky homes with the four hooves together, surveying the surrounding countryside.

They are diurnal and are most active in the early morning and late afternoons, but in cooler weather are active throughout the day. They are quite often solitary but usually in pairs, as they mate for life, or sometimes up to six loosely associated animals are encountered. They are territorial, actively chasing out any interlopers.

The tick species *Ixodes neitzi* parasitises klipspringers and is attracted to

KLIPSPRINGER

Gestation period: ± 220 days	
Young: one	
Mass: ♂ 10,5 kg, ♀ 13,5 kg.	
Shoulder height: 55 cm.	
Horns: 15 cm.	
Life expectancy: 15 years	

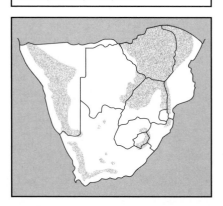

Left fore

Left hind

Actual size

territorial scent-marked bushes, climbing up to the marked point to await the animal's return to re-mark.

The voice is a loud piercing cry when in great danger, or a nasal whistle-like cry, repeated every 5 seconds when danger threatens. This may be as a duet by the male and female, is very sharp and directional and is probably to tell the predator that it has been spotted. Predators often give up the stalk and turn away on hearing this duetting call.

Enemies are leopards, caracal, hyaenas, baboons, black eagles, martial and crowned eagles. The young are taken by wildcats, pythons, monitor lizards and black-backed jackals. Only one altricial young is produced.

Common in suitable habitat

Food: They will often move away from their rocky habitat to forage, but will dash back at the least hint of danger. They are mainly browsers but also graze extensively. Will eat twigs, leaves, mosses, grasses and fruit, often standing up on their hind legs to reach succulent food. They are recorded as gnawing on old bones and eating termitaria soil, doubtless for the nutriments they contain. They are not dependent on water, assimilating all that is necessary from their diet. They will however drink, if water is available.

Distribution: SOUTH AFRICA: *Transvaal*: Ben Alberts, Borokalano, Doorndraai Dam, Hans Merensky, Hans Strydom Dam, Klaserie, Kruger Park, Lapalala, Londolozi, Loskop Dam, Mala Mala, Manyeleti, Messina, Nyala Ranch, Nylsvley, Ohrigstad Dam, Percy Fyfe, Pilanesberg, Rustenburg, Sabi-Sand, Sterkspruit, Timbavati, Umbabat/Motswari; *O.F.S.*: Maria Maroka; *Natal*: Giants Castle, Mkuzi, Phinda, Royal Natal, Umfolozi; *Cape*: Aughrabies, De Hoop, Gamkaberg, Gamkapoort, Hester Malan, Karoo, Mountain Zebra, Salmon's Dam.

SWAZILAND: Pongola; NAMIBIA: Daan Viljoen, Etosha, Naukluft, Von Bach, Waterberg Plateau; BOTSWANA: Gemsbok, Mashatu; ZIMBABWE: Chete, Chewore, Chizarira, Gonarhezhou, Hwange, Malapati, Matopos, Mana Pools, Matusadona, Nyanga; MOZAMBIQUE: Gorongosa.

Damara dik-dik

Madoqua kirkii

Damara dik-dik

66

Four species of dik-dik occur on the continent, but only one in our sub-region. These small, dainty antelope are best characterized by the curious trunk-like, elongated, mobile proboscis, tipped with open nostrils, which lack the ability to close as do the nostrils of some other antelope species. The mobile proboscis and mouthparts can extend in any direction to take in

DAMARA DIK-DIK

Gestation period: ± 170 days	
Young: one	
Mass: 5 kg.	
Shoulder height: 38 cm.	
Horns: 10 cm.	
Life expectancy: 9 years	

Left fore

Actual size

Left hind

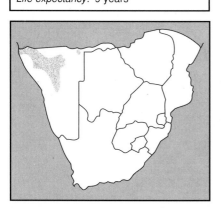

food. Preorbital glands, lying in front of the eyes, are large and conspicuous and are used for scent-marking. The hair on the forehead is long and can be raised in a crest when alarmed or in courtship. Only males have short horns which nearly follow the line of the face and are slightly forward curved at the tips. The hooves have hard, rubbery black pads on the back which are in contact with the ground. They act as shock-absorbers on the rocky terrain, the preferred habitat of the dik-diks.

They occur singly or in small family groups. When disturbed they give a short sharp explosive whistle and run for the deepest available cover and, if frightened, they may leap away in stiff-legged stotting bounces, emitting their sharp whistle with each bound. This sound is said to be the onomatapoeiac derivation of their name. Their usual vocalisation is a high-pitched, quavering whistle from their downward-extended nostrils. They are mainly diurnal with most activity at sunrise and late afternoon and dusk, with some crepuscular activity.

Their habitat is the dense woodland and thickets on stony ground in the more arid regions.

They are preyed upon by leopards, caracal, serval, African wild cat and large eagles, the young by monitor lizards and larger snakes. Only one young is born and little else is known of its reproductive habits.

Food: They are almost exclusively browsers, utilising almost all parts of the plant but young tender grass is sometimes eaten. To reach up to the tenderest parts of higher shrubs, they will stand on their hind feet, balancing against the shrub with their forelegs. Salt is important and the animals will die rapidly if it is not available. Water is not essential and the animals will subsist on the moisture from their food.

Distribution: NAMIBIA: Etosha, Kaudom, Von Bach, Waterberg Plateau. Two discrete populations of the Damara dik-dik occur on the continent. The other is in central east Africa, about 4 000 km north-east of the population in the sub-region.

Oribi
Ourebia ourebi
Oorbietjie

67

This monotypic species is a small beige antelope with pure white underparts, extending upwards over the rump to the base of the tail and high up the chest. It is distinguished from the smaller steenbok by the markings on its face and the bushy black-tipped tail. There is a pre-orbital round black gland on the face and a black spot just below the ears. The females lack

ORIBI

Gestation period: ± 220 days	
Young: one	
Mass: 15 kg.	
Shoulder height: 58 cm.	
Horns: 17 cm.	
Life expectancy: 12 years	

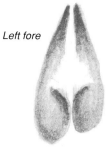

Left fore

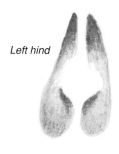

Left hind

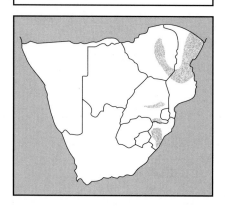

Actual size

horns, which on the males are straight and then curved forward at the tips.

They are usually solitary but may form herds of as many as 10 animals. Adult males are territorial. They lie up in grass with erect heads and keep a watchful eye out for danger. They are very inquisitive and will run off, stopping for a backwards look, even slowly returning. This often leads to their downfall. If suddenly disturbed they will bound off with a rocking-horse, stotting motion. The female appears to be more aware of danger and will take the lead in flight.

Their preferred habitat is open grasslands and floodplains, preferring short grass to long. They tend to choose slightly elevated land to rest on, as it offers better vantage. They avoid woodland, except margins, and are not present in forests or true desert.

Enemies are leopard, caracal, hyaena, African wild cat, and large eagles. Young are preyed upon by jackal, badger, baboon, monitor lizard and pythons. Only one precocial fawn is born.

Food: They are predominantly grazers, with a certain amount of browse taken. They do not drink, even if water is available, as their moisture is derived from their diet.

Distribution: SOUTH AFRICA: *Transvaal*: Kruger Park, Loskop Dam, Ohrigstad Dam, Rustenburg, Sterkspruit, Suikerbosrand; *O.F.S.*: Golden Gate; *Natal*: Giants Castle, Kamberg, Loteni, Oribi Gorge.

Very rare and localised

NAMIBIA: Eastern & Western Caprivi, Mahonga; BOTSWANA: Chobe; ZIMBABWE: Gonarhezhou; MOZAMBIQUE: Gorongosa.

Steenbok
Raphicerus campestris
Steenbok

68

These small antelopes are known elsewhere as 'steinbok', an unfortunate choice as 'steinbok' is the German name for the ibex (*Capra ibex*). They are widely distributed little animals, inhabitants of open country, not occurring in forest, dense woodland, rocky hills or mountains, and largely absent from desert regions, which they penetrate well in along watercourses with riparian bush. Only males carry horns. Steenbok are solitary except when the female is with a calf or, when in oestrus, is accompanied by a male. Usually diurnal in habit, they are most active during the mornings and late afternoons and, where persecuted, tend to nocturnal activity.

STEENBOK

Gestation period: ± 170 days

Young: one; rarely two

Mass: ♂ 11 kg, ♀ 12 kg.

Shoulder height: 50 cm.

Horns: 18 cm.

Life expectancy: 10 years

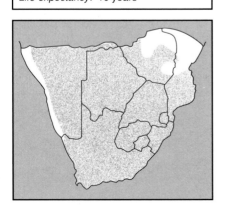

Left fore

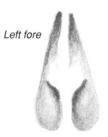

Actual size

Left hind

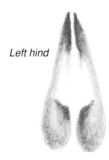

Both sexes are territorial and defend their areas against others. Serious fights are rare and juveniles make off when they see an adult. They have pre-orbital glands, showing as dark marks just in front of the eyes.

They lie flat to escape detection, hide in grass and will only flush at the last moment, running off rapidly, sometimes pausing momentarily to look back, before running on.

Their enemies are large and medium-sized carnivores, including caracal, African wild cat, jackal, badgers, pythons and martial eagles. The young are particularly susceptible. One precocial young, rarely two, is produced.

Food: They are mainly browsers but also graze.

Distribution: SOUTH AFRICA: *Transvaal*: Barberspan, Ben Alberts, Ben Lavin, Borokalano, Doorndraai Dam, Hans Merensky, Klaserie, Kruger Park, Langjan, Lapalala, Londolozi, Loskop Dam, Mala Mala, Manyeleti, Messina, Nyala Ranch, Nylsvley, Ohrigstad Dam, Percy Fyfe, Pilanesberg, Roodeplaat Dam, Rustenburg, Sabi-Sabi, Sabi-Sand, S A Lombard, Sterkspruit, Suikerbosrand, Timbavati, Umbabat/Motswari; *O.F.S.*: Erfenis Dam, Hendrik Verwoerd Dam, Maria Maroka, Soetdoring, Tussen-die-Riviere, Willem Pretorius; *Natal*: Hluhluwe, Mkuzi, Phinda, Royal Natal, St Lucia, Umfolozi, Weenen; *Cape*: Andries Vosloo, Aughrabies, Bontebok, Botsalano, De Hoop, Doornkloof, Gamkaberg, Gamkapoort, Hester Malan, Kalahari Gemsbok, Karoo, Kommandodrift, Langebaan, Mountain Zebra, Oviston, Rocher Pan, Rolfontein, Sandveld, Vaalbos.

SWAZILAND: Pongola; NAMIBIA: Daan Viljoen, Eastern & Western Caprivi, Etosha, Hardap Dam, Kaudom, Mahonga, Naukluft, Skeleton Coast, Von Bach, Waterberg Plateau; BOTSWANA: Central Kalahari, Chobe, Gemsbok, Khutse, Mabuasehube, Makgadikgadi, Mashatu, Moremi, Nxai Pan; ZIMBABWE: Gonarhezhou, Hwange, Matopos; MOZAMBIQUE: Maputo Elephant Park.

Common to very common, widespread

GRYSBOK

Two species of grysbok are found in the continent and both occur in the sub-region. Also known as the southern grysbok and the Cape grysbok, the grysbok is endemic to the southern Cape province, whereas the Sharpe's (or northern) grysbok occurs from southern Mozambique and Swaziland to just south of Lake Victoria. These small antelope are brown in colour but sprinkled throughout their coats, mainly on the upper parts, are innumerable white hairs which impart the grey streaky colour to their coats. These white hairs are largely absent from the neck, face, flanks and legs. Only the males carry horns which are short and, in the case of the Cape grysbok, rise vertically from the head, are slightly slanted forward and are longer than those of the Sharpe's grysbok. In the case of Sharpe's grysbok, the horns rise from the top of the head and slope slightly backwards and taper abruptly to a sharp point.

√ # Grysbok

Raphicerus melanotis

Grysbok

69

These secretive, nocturnal animals, commonly known as the Cape grysbok, are little-known because of their retiring habits. They differ from the Sharpe's grysbok in having supplementary or false hooves above their fetlocks, which are absent in Sharpe's grysbok. They are slightly larger and are not as distinctly reddish in colour. The back legs are slightly shorter than the forelegs, and this causes the backs of the animal to hunch. The preorbital gland is much larger than that of the Sharpe's grysbok. Only males carry horns.

Their predators are leopard and caracal and the young are taken by baboons and large snakes. Virtually nothing is known of their reproduction processes, but the young have a darker coat than the adult. Probably only one lamb is produced.

Food: Predominantly grazers, but will eat leaves and wild fruit. They are partial to the tender shoots and tendrils of grape vines and are regarded as pests where they occur in the Cape winelands.

Distribution: SOUTH AFRICA: *Cape*: Addo Elephant, Bontebok, De Hoop, Gamkaberg, Goukamma, Keurboom, Langebaan, Robberg, Thomas Baines, Zuurberg.

Actual size

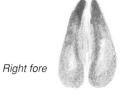

Right fore

Right hind

CAPE GRYSBOK	
Gestation period: ± 190 days	
Young: one	
Mass: 10,5 kg.	
Shoulder height: 50 cm.	
Horns: 11 cm.	
Life expectancy: unknown	

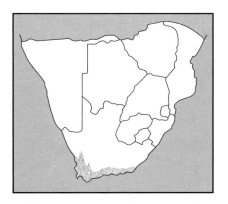

Left fore

*Actual
size*

Left hind

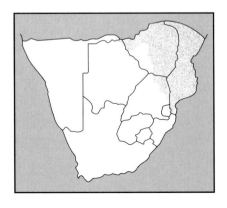

SHARPE'S GRYSBOK

Gestation period: ± 210 days	
Young: one	
Mass: 9 kg.	
Shoulder height: 50 cm.	
Horns: 10 cm.	
Life expectancy: unknown	

Sharpe's grysbok

Raphicerus sharpei

Sharpe se grysbok, *or* **Tropiese grysbok**

These are more common animals than the Cape grysbok. Nevertheless, because of their shy, retiring and usually nocturnal habit, are little known. The colour is a richer red than the Cape grysbok. There is a dark band extending from the rhinarium along the muzzle, which tapers and disap-

pears at about the level of the eyes. The eyes have a whitish ring and the sides of the face, from the rhinarium, are also whitish. The preorbital gland is much smaller and the underparts are lighter than in the Cape grysbok. Only males carry horns.

Sharpe's grysbok will graze in the cool late after-noons and they are, therefore, prey to both nocturnal and diurnal predators, such as lion, leopard, caracal, large raptors, pythons and others. Little is known of their reproduction habits. Probably only one lamb is produced.

Food: Mainly browsers on leaves and wild fruit, they will also eat tender new grass.

Distribution: SOUTH AFRICA: *Transvaal*: Hans Merensky, Hans Strydom Dam, Klaserie, Kruger Park, Sabi-Sabi, Sabi-Sand, Umbabat/Motswari.

Rare and patchily localised

ZIMBABWE: Chete, Chewore, Chizarira, Gonarhezhou, Hwange, Malapati, Mana Pools, Matusadona, Nyanga; MOZAMBIQUE: Gorongosa.

Suni

Neotragus moschatus

Soenie

Dwarf antelopes, suni are only about 35 cm at the shoulder, the male weighs a maximum of 5 - 5'/ kg and the female is slightly heavier. The sub-species of this region is a rich rufous-brown with a faint speckling along the upper parts. They have a conspicuous linear preorbital gland extending from the eye down the line of the face. Only the males have horns; these are widely spaced, follow the line of the face and are long and sharp. The maximum length is about 13 cm. They habitually wag their tails vigorously which often gives their presence away.

SUNI

Gestation period: ± 120 days	
Young: one	
Mass: ♂ 5 kg, ♀ 5,5 kg.	
Shoulder height: 35 cm.	
Horns: 13 cm.	
Life expectancy: 9 years	

Left fore

Left hind

Actual size

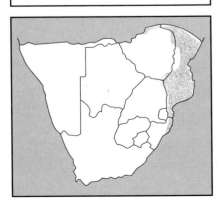

Preferred habitat is dry woodland, with thick underbrush and thickets. They are usually solitary, sometimes in pairs and more are known to congregate to graze together. Mainly diurnal, they are active mornings and afternoons, are very wary and, if surprised, will freeze for a long period before making off with a loud high-pitched 'tschee-tschee'. The male will bleat like a goat when pursuing the female.

Suni are relatively easy to trap because of their habit of using game paths. This trapping is consequently more depleting than predation by its natural enemies, which are many animal and large avian predators, as well as larger snakes.

Little is known of the reproduction habits of the suni, but one calf is produced.

Very rare and localised

Food: They are browsers, eating the young and tender shoots of trees and shrubs, also mushrooms, fallen fruit, weeds and occasionally grass and field crops. They are not dependent on water, getting all they need from their diet.

Distribution: SOUTH AFRICA: *Transvaal:* Kruger Park; *Natal:* False Bay, Mkuzi, Ndumu, Phinda, St Lucia.

SWAZILAND: Pongola; ZIMBABWE: Gonarhezhou, Mana Pools; MOZAMBIQUE: Gorongosa.

IMPALA

Two impala sub-species are recorded. The difference between the two lies in the dark blaze down the face of the black-faced impala, its darker and different colouration and its greater mass. The black-faced impala occurs only in the north west of Namibia and into Angola and is an uncommon animal. By far the most common is the beautiful and graceful impala, which is common in its habitat. Its range extends as far north as northern Kenya.

/ Impala

Aepyceros melampus melampus

Rooibok

72

The lighter but not the smaller of the two sub-species, more richly coloured and by far the most common antelope in the sub-region. In common with the black-faced impala is the presence on the lower back legs of the distinctive, conspicuous, oval tufts of black hair, like 'socks', overlying metatarsal

IMPALA

Gestation period: ± 195 days	
Young: one	
Mass: ♂ 55 kg, ♀ 40 kg.	
Shoulder height: ♂ 90 cm, ♀ 85 cm.	
Horns: 80 cm.	
Life expectancy: 12 years	

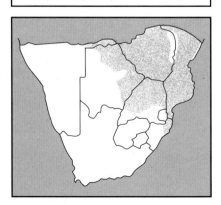

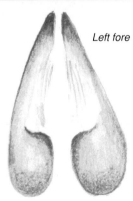

Left fore

Actual size

Left hind

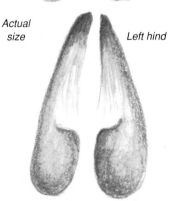

glands in the skin. On the stern of the males is a small bare glandular patch which secretes an oily substance. Only males have horns, lyrate in shape, maximum length about 80 cm.

Form large breeding herds of up to 100, or even in exceptional cases up to 200, but more usually up to 20. These consist of young, females and sub-adult males, attended by a watchful, dominant male, or in larger herds, two males, watchfully aloof from the herd. Potentially dominant males form juvenile and young adult bachelor herds, which generally keep away from the breeding herd. At times of rut the bachelor adults become restless, often leaving the herd to form their own breeding herd. With much roaring and aggression they may disrupt a breeding herd, for possession of which they challenge and fight the dominant males.

They are diurnal animals, but the dominant male will graze little in the day, preferring to stay alert and grazing mainly at night. Their voice is a harsh warning barking snort, bellowing and grunting in rut and a soft bleating by the calves in contact with the mother, or louder when lost.

Impala are the major food component of the larger predators where they occur mutually, such as lion, leopard, cheetah, hunting dog, spotted hyaena and the crocodile. Young are taken by the larger eagles, pythons and jackals. The females bear a single calf in isolation from the herd in thick bush or tall grass and eat the afterbirth. The whole crop of births takes place together. Young are hidden for a day or two and are usually able to join the herd with their mother 24 hours after birth, otherwise they are kept hidden for a few days. Remain with the herd about 15 months, after which the males are driven out to join the bachelor groups.

Food: Browse and graze; in dry seasons tend to congregate in greener riverine areas. Eat tender tip twigs and leaves of shrubs and trees, favouring acacias. Depend upon availability of water and the presence of a herd is usually evidence of nearby water.

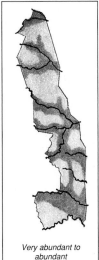

Very abundant to abundant

Distribution: SOUTH AFRICA: *Transvaal*: Ben Alberts, Ben Lavin, Blyde River Canyon, Borokalano, Doorndraai Dam, Hans Merensky, Klaserie, Kruger Park, Langjan, Lapalala, Londolozi, Loskop Dam, Mala Mala, Manyeleti, Messina, Nyala Ranch, Nylsvley, Percy Fyfe, Pilanesberg, Roodeplaat Dam, Rustenburg, Sabi-Sabi, Sabi-Sand, S A Lombard, Timbavati, Umbabat/Motswari; *O.F.S.*: Soetdoring, Tussen-die-Riviere, Willem Pretorius; *Natal*: Hluhluwe, Itala, Kenneth Stainbank, Mkuzi, Ndumu, Phinda, St Lucia, Umfolozi; *Cape*: Botsalano, Mkambati, Thomas Baines, Vaalbos; SWAZILAND: Pongola.

NAMIBIA: Daan Viljoen, Eastern & Western Caprivi, Waterberg Plateau; BOTSWANA: Chobe, Makgadikgadi, Mashatu, Moremi, Nxai Pan; ZIMBABWE: Chete, Chewore, Chizarira, Gonarhezhou, Hwange, Malapati, Matopos, Mana Pools, Matusadona; MOZAMBIQUE: Gorongosa

BLACK-FACED IMPALA

Gestation period: ± 195 days	
Young: one	
Mass: ♂ 62 kg, ♀ 50 kg.	
Shoulder height: 90 cm.	
Horns: 65 cm.	
Life expectancy: 12 years	

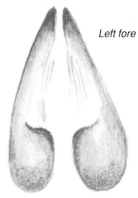

Left fore

Actual size

Left hind

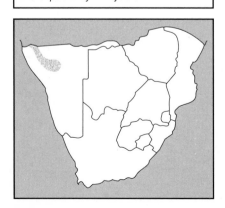

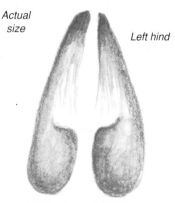

Black-faced impala
Aepyceros melampus petersi
Swartneusrooibok

73

Appearance similar to the impala, colouration differs in being darker and the upper parts of the body lacking the rich reddish brown, being duller brown with a purplish sheen. Tips of the ears darker and tails considerably longer and bushier. There is a very dark stripe from the nostril to the top of the head, wide up to the eyes and narrow to the top of the head, which is characteristic.

Because they are far less numerous than the impala, herd congregations are correspondingly smaller. Herds usually number up to 20 but more in lambing times, splitting up afterwards. The social behaviour and structure is similar. Their habitat is dense riverine, where they tend to remain during the day. Available water is vital.

Reproduction as the impala. Records reveal that, in the event of the births of twins, one is totally ignored and allowed to die.

Food: Similar to the impala. Seasonally they eat large quantities of pods of the acacias. They compete with goats for available food and their existence is threatened by the increasing competition from these problem animals.

Distribution: NAMIBIA: Etosha.

Grey rhebok
Pelea capreolus
Vaalribbok

74

The name rhebok probably originated when the early settlers saw in the animal a likeness to the roebuck (roe deer). This name evolved over time to the present spelling. They usually live in small parties of up to 20 animals, with various other groupings including solitary males and family groups. These slender and graceful antelopes are associated with rocky mountain slopes and plateaux and rocky hills with good grass cover. The dominant male will defend its territory from encroachment with an exaggerated display, which usually sends the other animal on its way. Only males carry horns which are almost straight but curve slightly forward.

Three vocalisations have been noted, these are: moaning, snorting and hissing. The snorting by either sex can continue for a long while until the

GREY RHEBOK

Gestation period: ± 260 days	
Young: one, sometimes two	
Mass: 20 kg.	
Shoulder height: 75 cm.	
Horns: 28cm.	
Life expectancy: 9 years	

Left fore

Actual size

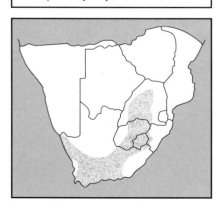

Left hind

Very rare and localised

source of their concern is identified. They are accomplished jumpers, able to leap gracefully over quite high obstacles. They make off with a rocking-horse motion, rather like that of the reedbuck. In their direct and swerving, swift flight, their 'white flag' undertail is prominently displayed.

Their enemies are leopard, caracal, and for the young also jackal, baboon and eagle. One, sometimes two calves are born.

Food: They are both browsers and grazers, with grass being the major component. They do not appear to be dependent upon surface water.

Distribution: SOUTH AFRICA: *Transvaal*: Kruger Park, Ohrigstad Dam, Pilanesberg, Sterkspruit, Suikerbosrand; *O.F.S.*: Golden Gate, Maria Maroka; *Natal*: Giants Castle, Kamberg, Loteni, Royal Natal; *Cape*: Bontebok, De Hoop, Gamkaberg, Gamkapoort, Karoo, Mountain Zebra, Oviston, Salmon's Dam, Vaalbos, Zuurberg.

Roan
Hippotragus equinus
Bastergemsbok

75

The name roan refers to the animal's colour which has a strawberry tint in a certain light. The Afrikaans name Bastergemsbok (bastard gemsbok) seems unfortunate for such a magnificent and regal antelope and, although closely related to the gemsbok, it is sufficiently far removed in appearance not to warrant the nominal association. They are surpassed in size only by the eland which, unlike the graceful roan, is a lumbering ox-like animal. Both sexes carry horns with those of the female being lighter and shorter.

These gregarious animals usually associate in small herds of 5 to 12 up to 25 animals, but aggregations of up to 80 animals are not uncommon, these, however, are temporary associations. The herds are stable, characteristically remaining in the same activity area for long periods, 8 years having been recorded in Kruger Park and 30 years in East Africa. Dominant bulls in these activity areas defend the females against the attention of other males. Strange bulls challenging the dominant bull will be subject to high intensity clashing of their stout powerful horns, pushing and lunging from a kneeling position. These particular bouts rarely result in serious injury and the bout terminates when one or the other yields. They are, however, very powerful and dangerous animals and other more serious fights can often

ROAN

Gestation period: ± 275 days	
Young: one	
Mass: ♂ 280 kg, ♀ 250 kg.	
Shoulder height: ♂ 155 cm, ♀ 145 cm.	
Horns: 90 cm.	
Life expectancy: 17 years	

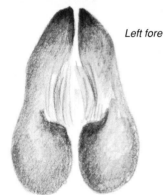

Left fore

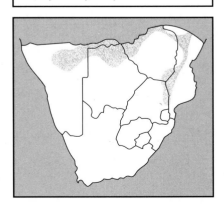

¹⁄₃ actual size

Left hind

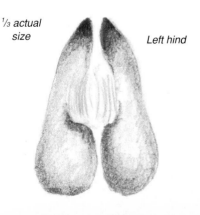

end fatally for one of the contestants. Hunters are also in severe danger from these powerful animals. The major action in the fight is a violent backward sweep of the horns.

The preferred habitat is lightly wooded savannah with extensive open grassy areas with available water. They are sensitive to habitat change and very specific in their requirement. As a result their occurrence is discontinuous in the subregion.

Their vocalisation is a horse-like snort when alarmed, otherwise mainly silent. If attacked will defend themselves bravely with sweeps of their sharp, stout horns.

Enemies are lion, leopard, spotted hyaena, wild dog and crocodile. They flee in file with sideways waving tails. Only one precocial calf is produced.

Food: When feeding they tend to scatter, giving the effect of a lack of cohesion. They are predominantly grazers, which browse only a small proportion of their food. Will readily turn to browsing when grazing is poor and, therefore, remain in better condition than the sable, which do not readily browse.

Distribution: SOUTH AFRICA: *Transvaal*: Doorndraai Dam, Hans Strydom Dam, Klaserie, Kruger Park, Lapalala, Nylsvley, Percy Fyfe, Pilanesberg; *Cape*: Vaalbos.

NAMIBIA: Eastern & Western Caprivi, Etosha, Kaudom, Mahonga, Waterberg Plateau; BOTSWANA: Chobe, Makgadikgadi, Moremi, Nxai Pan; ZIMBABWE: Chete, Chewore, Chizarira, Gonarhezhou, Hwange, Malapati, Matopos, Mana Pools, Matusadona.

Rare and localised

Sable
Hippotragus niger
Swartwitpens

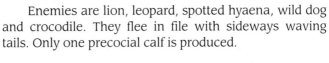

76

Again a rather undignified Afrikaans name, Swartwitpens (black, white belly), for another of the lordly *Hippotragus* tribe. These startlingly beautiful animals stand out in their habitat of grassland, particularly when winter colours the veld beige. The name sable reflects the colour of the beast, although only the adult males develop the black, satiny sheen to their coats. The other animals are a dark reddish brown, but old females become very dark brown, almost black, like the males. The belly and facial markings are a pure white, contrasting with the dark colour of the rest of the body.

Although smaller and more slender than the roans, the sables are,

SABLE

Gestation period: ± 275 days	
Young: one	
Mass: ♂ 250 kg, ♀ 210 kg.	
Shoulder height: ♂ 120 cm, ♀ 90 cm.	
Horns: 150 cm.	
Life expectancy: 17 years	

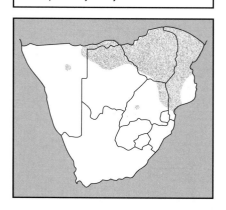

Left fore

¹/₂ *actual size*

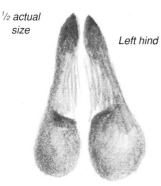

Left hind

nevertheless, majestic animals. Their long, swept-back horns are the longest of any antelope species, excepting the kudu. Both sexes have horns with those of the females shorter and more slender than those of the male.

Sable are gregarious, diurnal inhabitants of savannah woodland with available water. They prefer open sparse woodland with vleis and good stands of grass. They live in herds of up to 30 animals, forming temporary aggregations of sometimes more than 170. They are territorial animals, with a dominant bull which defends its territory and whose show of threat usually leads to the retreat of any interloper. If not, fighting occurs which may turn into a serious encounter. They usually fight kneeling, with sweeps of their sharp powerful horns, which can result in the death of one of the combatants. Hunters are also in danger from the horns of this great antelope. Like the roans, one or two females may secure dominance within a herd and are responsible for herd welfare. They do, however, remain subservient to the dominant male. Voice is similar to the roan.

Their enemies are as the roans. They flee in a closed troop. Only one precocial calf is produced.

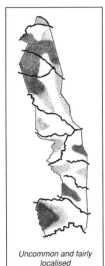

Uncommon and fairly localised

Food: They are predominantly grazers but will take some browse, especially in the drier seasons. They are dependent upon available water.

Distribution: SOUTH AFRICA: *Transvaal*: Ben Alberts, Ben Lavin, Borokalano, Doorndraai Dam, Hans Merensky, Hans Strydom Dam, Klaserie, Kruger Park, Lapalala, Loskop Dam, Mala Mala, Manyeleti, Messina, Percy Fyfe, Pilanesberg, Roodeplaat Dam, Rustenburg, Umbabat/Motswari; *Cape*: Vaalbos.

NAMIBIA: Eastern & Western Caprivi, Kaudom, Mahonga, Waterberg Plateau; BOTSWANA: Chobe, Makgadikgadi, Moremi, Nxai Pan; ZIMBABWE: Chete, Chewore, Chizarira, Gonarhezhou, Hwange, Malapati, Mana Pools, Matusadona, Matopos, Nyanga; MOZAMBIQUE: Gorongosa.

Gemsbok
Oryx gazella
Gemsbok

77

This inhabitant of more arid country once roamed large parts of the continent. The advance of man's influence has seen shrinkage of at least 2/3 of the range of these animals. They are predominantly diurnal, with some activity on moonlit nights. Their habitat is desert and semi-desert, with open savannah and bush savannah. They will penetrate fairly thick bush savannah, but this is usually when in search of open country within that area.

Gemsbok in the Gemsbok National Park

Gemsbok are gregarious animals forming herds of up to 12 animals and smaller bachelor herds. In seasons of plenty they tend to congregate into larger herds, breaking up as the season degenerates.

They are territorial, with a dominant bull controlling a territory much larger than that of any other ungulate.

They have a specialised metabolism to allow them to survive the high heat and dryness. The temperature in their habitat needs to rise very high before the gemsbok begins to sweat. This conserves body-moisture. However, when the temperature rises above the critical level, where cooling through sweating is necessary, the animals then sweat profusely. Furthermore, mechanisms in the brain ensure that the blood circulating there remains substantially cooler than in the rest of the body. Both sexes carry horns, with those of the female being longer and thinner.

Enemies are lion, leopard, hunting dog, and for the young, hyaena, cheetah, serval, caracal, jackal. Man is the major threat to the gemsbok. One precocial young is produced, rarely twins.

Food: They are predominantly grazers, but will also browse the shoots and leaves of trees, eat desert melons and tubers. Will drink water if available and will dig for it, but rely on their food for moisture.

Distribution: SOUTH AFRICA: *Transvaal*: Ben Alberts, Langjan, Lapalala, Nyala Ranch, Pilanesberg, S A Lombard; *O.F.S.*: Bloemhof Dam, Maria Maroka, Soetdoring, Tussen-die-Riviere, Willem Pretorius; *Cape*: Aughrabies, Botsalano, Hester Malan, Kalahari Gemsbok, Karoo, Mkambati, Rolfontein, Sandveld, Vaalbos.

NAMIBIA: Daan Viljoen, Etosha, Hardap Dam, Kaudom, Naukluft, Skeleton Coast, Von Bach, Waterberg Plateau; BOTSWANA: Central Kalahari, Chobe, Gemsbok, Khutse, Mabuasehube, Makgadikgadi, Moremi, Nxai Pan; ZIMBABWE: Hwange.

Left fore

½ actual size

Left hind

GEMSBOK
Gestation period: ± 260 days
Young: one, rarely two
Mass: ♂ 235 kg, ♀ 210 kg.
Shoulder height: 120 cm.
Horns: 110 cm.
Life expectancy: 20 years

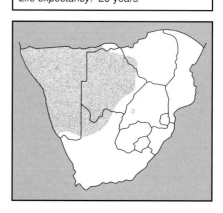

BUFFALO

In South Africa the relict population in the Addo Elephant Park is morphologically slightly different to the other populations and is kept separate. They are free of foot and mouth disease and rinderpest and the authorities do not allow importation to the area of any other stock which may introduce these diseases.

Buffalo
Syncerus caffer
Buffel

78

These large, ox-like bovids have a reputation for savagery and cunning and not without reason. Despite the fact that they are solely vegetarian, they are responsible for the deaths of many people throughout the continent and are rightly feared by all with whom they come into contact. The animals are quick-tempered and will not hesitate to use their massive horns to ram and to gore if they perceive any threat whatsoever. Their reputation for extreme cunning and the circling around to wait in ambush for a hunter following their trail, is probably much exaggerated. This may occur only if the animal is seriously wounded.

They are generally most active in the evening, night and morning, resting up in the shade during the heat of the day. They are gregarious and can congregate in massive herds of in excess of a thousand animals, sometimes as many as three thousand. These large aggregations are, however, rare because of the shrinkage in populations over the years and, in particular because of the massive destruction of the animals in the rinderpest plague which swept down from the north in the nineteenth century. Large herds are now only encountered in Botswana and, to a lesser extent, in Zimbabwe.

Old bulls and young males move off and form bachelor herds, some old males move away to become solitary and are most prone to lion predation. Within the herd there is a clearly defined linear dominance and, the smaller the herd, the more clearly it is defined and jealously maintained. They are usually fairly quiet and their voice is generally confined to grunting. Calves bleat and males will bellow hoarsely during battle and will paw the ground and kick back the earth.

They need grass and shade and a plentiful supply of water, as they generally drink twice daily and will avoid areas where these three criteria are not met. They will, however, range far from water in search of suitable habitat and grazing. Mud-wallowing is important for thermo-regulation.

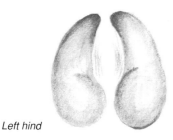

Left fore

¹/₄ actual size

Left hind

BUFFALO

Gestation period: ± 340 days	
Young: one, very rarely two	
Mass: ♂ 800 kg, ♀ 700 kg.	
Shoulder height: 160 cm.	
Horns: 120 cm.	
Life expectancy: 22 years	

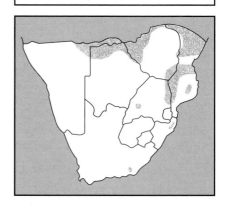

Common and widespread

Their main predators are lions. Young, sick and weak are also taken by wild dogs and spotted hyaenas. A single calf is produced and rarely twins are born.

Food: They are almost exclusively grazers, but will take a small amount of browse. The heat of the day causes them to stop feeding and they will retire to shade to ruminate. Most feeding is at night

Distribution: SOUTH AFRICA: *Transvaal*: Klaserie, Kruger Park, Londolozi, Loskop Dam, Mala Mala, Manyeleti, Percy Fyfe, Pilanesberg, Sabi-Sabi, Sabi-Sand, Timbavati, Umbabat/Motswari; *O.F.S.*: Golden Gate, Willem Pretorius; Natal ; Hluhluwe, Ndumu, St Lucia, Umfolozi, Weenen; *Cape*: Addo Elephant, Andries Vosloo, Thomas Baines, Vaalbos.

NAMIBIA: Eastern & Western Caprivi, Kaudom, Mahonga, Naukluft, Waterberg Plateau; BOTSWANA: Chobe, Gemsbok, Makgadikgadi, Moremi, Nxai Pan; ZIMBABWE: Chete, Chewore, Chizarira, Gonarhezhou, Hwange, Malapati, Matopos, Mana Pools, Matusadona; MOZAMBIQUE: Gorongosa.

√ Kudu
Tragelaphus strepsiceros
Koedoe

79

Few could be unimpressed with the regal bearing of these large, lordly antelopes of the African veld. A fully grown male can weigh up to 250 kg and the female up to 200 kg. Characteristic of the males are the beautiful, symmetrical spiral horns with a maximum length in excess of 1.75 metres. Generally only the males carry horns, very rarely the females, which horns are usually thin and deformed. Like the related bushbucks the horns have a well-developed ridge following the curvature of the spiral. This graceful spiral has a disadvantage for the animal in certain circumstances and it is tragic to find two dead males inextricably caught together by interlocked horns after a battle.

Kudu need scrubby woodland for food and protection, and are not found in open grassland or desert areas. They particularly favour areas with rocky, broken terrain with water nearby. In more arid areas they congregate along water courses. They are diurnal animals, most active in the morning and late afternoons, resting under shelter in the heat of the day. Their warning cry, a harsh bark, is described as the loudest of any antelope species. They run with their heads level to the ground, the horns laid back to avoid them being tangled in branches.

Left fore

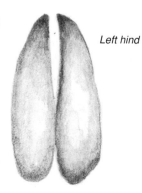

¹/₂ actual size

Left hind

KUDU	
Gestation period: ± 215 days	
Young: one	
Mass: ♂ 220 kg, ♀ 180 kg.	
Shoulder height: ♂ 150 cm, ♀ 135 cm.	
Horns: 160 cm.	
Life expectancy: 14 years	

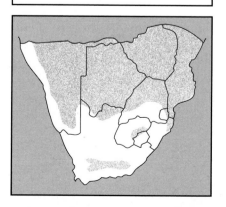

Small family groups are formed of generally not more than twelve animals, consisting generally of females and calves, with the males joining the group only for the purpose of mating. The males form their own bachelor groups or range solitary.

Their principal predators are leopard, hunting dog, cheetah and lion. The female gives birth to only a single calf, usually after mid summer when the grass is at its tallest. When birthing is due the female leaves the herd and the single calf is born in the cover of the long grass. The mother then eats the afterbirth.

Food: Kudu are almost exclusively browsers, but sometimes eat grass. Food variety is greater than for other antelope species. An over-population of kudu in a restricted habitat, and the consequent pressure on available food, can trigger a defense mechanism in the plants, causing them to drastically increase the production of tannin in the leaves. This is poisonous to the animals and frequently causes mortality in these confined areas.

Common and
widespread

Distribution: SOUTH AFRICA: *Transvaal*: Ben Alberts, Ben Lavin, Blyde River Canyon, Borokalano, Doorndraai Dam, Hans Merensky, Hans Strydom Dam, Klaserie, Kruger Park, Langjan, Lapalala, Londolozi, Loskop Dam, Mala Mala, Manyeleti, Messina, Nyala Ranch, Nylsvley, Ohrigstad Dam, Percy Fyfe, Pilanesberg, Roodeplaat Dam, Rustenburg, Sabi-Sabi, Sabi-Sand, Suikerbosrand, Timbavati, Umbabat/Motswari; *O.F.S.*: Tussen-die-Riviere, Willem Pretorius; *Natal*: Hluhluwe, Itala, Mkuzi, Ndumu, Phinda, St Lucia, Umfolozi, Weenen; *Cape*: Addo Elephant, Andries Vosloo, Aughrabies, Botsalano, Doornkloof, Gamkapoort, Kalahari Gemsbok, Karoo, Kommandodrift, Mkambati, Mountain Zebra, Oviston, Rolfontein, Thomas Baines, Vaalbos, Zuurberg; SWAZILAND: Pongola.

NAMIBIA: Daan Viljoen, Eastern & Western Caprivi, Etosha, Hardap Dam, Kaudom, Mahonga, Naukluft, Skeleton Coast, Von Bach, Waterberg Plateau; BOTSWANA: Central Kalahari, Chobe, Gemsbok, Khutse, Mabuasehube, Makgadikgadi, Mashatu, Moremi, Nxai Pan; ZIMBABWE: Chete, Chewore, Chizarira, Gonarhezhou, Hwange, Malapati, Matopos, Mana Pools, Matusadona, Nyanga; MOZAMBIQUE: Gorongosa.

Sitatunga

Tragelaphus spekei

Waterkoedoe

The Afrikaans name is appropriate, as the horns of this member of the bushbuck family are similar to those of the kudu, and they are creatures of swampy places. They are widely distributed in their restricted habitat type, through tropical and equatorial central west Africa. In this sub-region they are, however, restricted to the swamps of northern Botswana and the Caprivi.

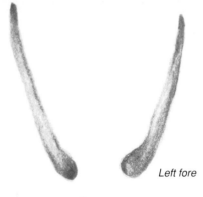

Left fore

SITATUNGA

Gestation period: ± 225 days	
Young: one, rarely twins	
Mass: ♂ 115 kg, ♀ 55 kg.	
Shoulder height: ♂ 115 cm, ♀ 90 cm.	
Horns: 90 cm.	
Life expectancy: 19 years	

½ actual size

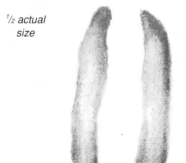

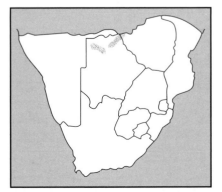

Left hind

They are considerably larger than the bushbuck and in appearance are like long-legged bushbuck. Adult males are a drab brown colour, sometimes with indistinct yellowish blotches on the mid-back, with no vertical stripes. Only the males have horns. The females are distinctly smaller and their colour varies considerably, from dark brown to a reddish brown, with a dark dorsal band with four transverse white stripes and white haunch spots. The hair of both sexes is shaggy and silky. They have two transverse white markings on the neck and the head has a white chevron mark between the eyes, with a white spot below the base of the ears.

Their long narrow hooves are specially adapted to their aquatic habitat. The lobes or claws splay out, allowing purchase on dense reedmats, mud, sand and dense waterweed.

They are shy and secretive, both diurnal and nocturnal, resting in the hottest part of the day and venturing out at night onto the surrounding plains to feed, returning to the swamps just before dawn. This movement is early in the evening in undisturbed areas, but where there is interference, such as in the lower parts of the Okavango swamps, they will venture beyond the confines of their swampy habitat only very late at night.

They are excellent swimmers, sometimes swimming with just their nostrils exposed. In danger they will always make for the waters of the swamp. Their voice is like that of the bushbuck; the male has a nocturnal sneezing call and the alarm call is a lowing. Their predators are crocodiles, lion and leopard and the young are taken by pythons. Excessive flooding may drown the young.

Sitatunga form small herds of about six individuals, comprising a male, with several females and juveniles. One, rarely two young are produced.

Food: Swamp and water vegetation, young grass from surrounding areas and field crops from raided farms.

Distribution: NAMIBIA: Eastern & Western Caprivi, Mahonga; BOTSWANA: Chobe, Moremi.

√ Nyala

Tragelaphus angasii

Njala

81

Once known as the Angas' bushbuck, after their discoverer, Mr Douglas Angas, these medium-sized antelopes are associated with proximity to thickets, from which they rarely stray far. They favour patchy woodland country or floodplain, preferably with available water, although independent

Left fore

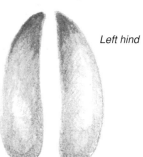

Left hind

$^2/_3$ actual size

NYALA	
Gestation period: ± 255 days	
Young: one	
Mass: ♂ 110 kg, ♀ 75 kg.	
Shoulder height: ♂ 110 cm, ♀ 95 cm.	
Horns: 80 cm.	
Life expectancy: 15 years	

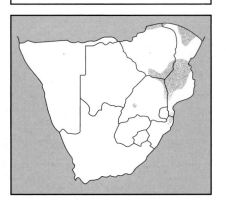

of its constant availability. Males are like shaggy, dark kudu bulls and females resemble female kudu. They are smaller than the kudu and larger than the bushbuck. The most distinguishing characteristic is their yellow legs. Only males have horns, which are less spiralled than those of the kudu and which are white-tipped. The males will display aggressively when others appear to threaten. They will raise the dorsal crest of white hair along the back, raise the head high, moving slowly, and deliberately lifting the legs higher than normal. Further display development sees the tail raised over the rump, the ventral white hairs fanned out and the head lowered with the horns pointed outwards.

Mainly diurnal, they will tend to become secretive and nocturnal if pressured by hunting. They are gregarious and form herds of up to 30 animals but usually occur in two's or three's. Groups usually comprise a female and her offspring. They often join up to form large female groups, which may be joined at feeding grounds by male groups.

They are predominantly browsers, with fruit dislodged by the primates, twigs and leaves. New grass is also relished.

Their main enemy is the leopard. They are taken also by lion and crocodile. The young are preyed upon by the smaller predators and also baboon. At breeding time the female will be joined by several males from the bachelor groups. This will last for only two to three days while the female is in oestrus. A single calf is born.

Common in suitable
habitat

Distribution: SOUTH AFRICA: *Transvaal*: Ben Alberts, Ben Lavin, Klaserie, Kruger Park, Langjan, Lapalala, Londolozi, Loskop Dam, Mala Mala, Manyeleti, Messina, Nyala Ranch, Sabi-Sabi, Sabi-Sand, Timbavati, Umbabat Motswari; *Natal*: Hluhluwe, Kenneth Stainbank, Mkuzi, Ndumu, Phinda, St Lucia, Umfolozi; SWAZILAND: Pongola.

ZIMBABWE: Chewore, Gonarhezhou, Mana Pools; MOZAMBIQUE: Gorongosa, Maputo Elephant.

√ Bushbuck
Tragelaphus scriptus
Bosbok

82

By nature the fairly common bushbuck are solitary, rather silent and secretive antelopes which inhabit dense riverine bush adjacent to permanent water courses. Solitary males and females are most frequently encountered, although they may sometimes form small groups of females, sub-adult

Left fore

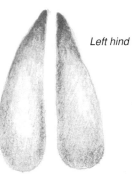

Left hind

Actual size

BUSHBUCK	
Gestation period: ± 180 days	
Young: one	
Mass: ♂ 60 kg, ♀ 35 kg.	
Shoulder height: ♂ 80 cm, ♀ 70 cm.	
Horns: 52 cm.	
Life expectancy: 12 years	

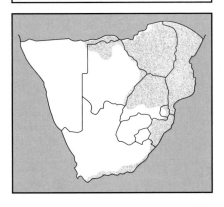

males and young. The males sometimes form bachelor herds of as many as nine individuals. They are also found near suburbia of even the larger towns and cities.

Three sub-species occur in our region, with the southernmost animals being the darkest in colour with fewer spots on their flanks and no transverse lines on the back. The intermediate sub-species is lighter but without transverse lines. The northernmost animal, commonly known as the 'Chobe bushbuck', is the most attractive of the three. The adult Chobe male is a rich chestnut colour, strongly marked with transverse body lines and spots on the flanks. The two greyish neck-markings stand out prominently on older specimens.

Their warning is a harsh bark, with that of the male being the harshest. To maintain contact in the dense bush they utter grunts. They are also adept and tireless swimmers.

Cornered bushbuck can be extremely dangerous, using their sharp horns and wicked hooves to good effect. Only the males have horns and these are short, straight and sharp. In the battle for dominance they frequently fight to the death with other males. Leopards are known to have been killed or put to flight by an enraged bushbuck.

Their principal predator is the leopard. They are sometimes prey to lion, caracal and crocodiles. The young are taken also by smaller predators and by pythons. A single calf is produced which is hidden in dense bush. The mother returns periodically to suckle it until it is able to fend for itself.

Food: Bushbuck are mainly browsers but will occasionally graze. They readily adapt to other forms of food, to the point of being a nuisance. Vegetable and ornamental gardens are raided and young trees in plantations are damaged.

Distribution: SOUTH AFRICA: *Transvaal*: Ben Alberts, Blyde River Canyon, Borokalano, Doorndraai Dam, Hans Merensky, Hans Strydom Dam, Klaserie, Kruger Park, Langjan, Lapalala, Londolozi, Loskop Dam, Mala Mala, Manyeleti, Messina, Nyala Ranch, Nylsvley, Ohrigstad Dam, Percy Fyfe, Pilanesberg, Rustenburg, Sabi-Sabi, Sabi-Sand, Sterkspruit, Timbavati, Umbabat/Motswari; *O.F.S.*: Willem Pretorius; *Natal*: False Bay, Giants Castle, Hluhluwe, Kenneth Stainbank, Loteni, Mkuzi, Phinda, Ndumu, Oribi Gorge, Royal Natal, St Lucia, Umfolozi, Weenen; *Cape*: Addo Elephant, Andries Vosloo, Goukamma, Keurboom, Thomas Baines, Tsitsikamma Coastal, Tsitsikamma Forest, Zuurberg.

SWAZILAND: Pongola; BOTSWANA: Chobe, Mashatu, Moremi; NAMIBIA: Eastern & Western Caprivi, Mahonga; ZIMBABWE: Chete, Chewore, Chizarira, Gonarhezhou, Hwange, Malapati, Matopos, Mana Pools, Matusadona, Nyanga; MOZAMBIQUE: Gorongosa, Maputo Elephant.

Widespread, common in suitable habitat

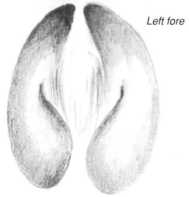

Left fore

ELAND	
Gestation period: ± 260 days	
Young: one, rarely two	
Mass: ♂ 700 kg, ♀ 450 kg.	
Shoulder height: ♂ 170 cm, ♀ 150 cm.	
Horns: 100 cm.	
Life expectancy: 20 years	

⅓ actual size

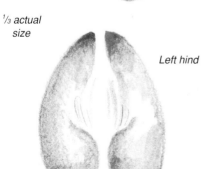

Left hind

Eland

Taurotragus oryx

Eland

83

Eland are the largest antelope, almost ox-like in appearance and temperament. The mass can be in excess of 750 kg. The colour is generally a beige and animals from the more northern parts of the sub-region have vertical body stripes. The neck and shoulders are a greyish colour in older animals, which is actually the colour of the skin showing through the hair which has worn thin. Both sexes have horns, with those of the female not being as heavy as those of the male. The forehead has a tuft of matted dark-brown hair, which smells strongly, due to a secretion from glands at the base.

Their favoured habitat is open savannah country, semi-desert and montane grasslands. They are timid, gregarious animals, mainly diurnal, occurring in small herds, but sometimes aggregations of many animals are encountered, even as many as a thousand animals. Herds of up to twelve adult males are not uncommon. They are generally territorial. Males meet with lowered head and push and shove with horns interlocking, during which time fatalities may occur. Females act similarly but on a much lesser scale. They will not tolerate strange calves, which are repelled with considerable vigour by a sideways swiping of their horns. They are mainly silent, but will puff and grunt like cattle when feeding. Females will moo to communicate with the calves, which bleat in response or whimper if they are stressed.

When adult eland walk they produce the classical 'clicking' sound which is attributed to the movement in the carpel bones in their knees. They are adept at jumping despite their size, being able to clear two metres with ease. They are also fast runners. Because of their docility and the quality of their meat and milk, they are being increasingly domesticated. The major predators are lion and hunting dog, with the foals subject to predation by leopards, spotted hyaena and cheetah. They produce one and rarely two young.

Fairly common in certain areas

Food: They are predominantly browsers, but are also partial to freshly sprouted grass. They are not too dependent upon water but will drink if it is available.

Distribution: SOUTH AFRICA: *Transvaal*: Ben Alberts, Borokalano, Kruger Park, Lapalala, Loskop Dam, Manyeleti, Messina, Nylsvley, Ohrigstad Dam, Pilanesberg, Rustenburg, S A Lombard, Suikerbosrand; *O.F.S.*: Bloemhof Dam, Golden Gate,

Soetdoring, Tussen-die-Riviere, Willem Pretorius; *Natal*: Giants Castle, Itala, Kamberg, Loteni, Ndumu, Oribi Gorge, Royal Natal, Weenen; *Cape*: Addo Elephant, Amalinda, Andries Vosloo, Aughrabies, Botsalano, De Hoop, Kalahari Gemsbok, Oviston, Rolfontein, Sandveld, Thomas Baines, Vaalbos, Zuurberg.

NAMIBIA: Daan Viljoen, Etosha, Hardap Dam, Kaudom, Naukluft, Von Bach, Waterberg Plateau; BOTSWANA: Central Kalahari, Chobe, Gemsbok, Khutse, Mabuasehube, Makgadikgadi, Mashatu; ZIMBABWE: Chete, Chewore, Chizarira, Gonarhezhou, Hwange, Matopos, Nyanga; MOZAMBIQUE: Gorongosa, Maputo Elephant.

REEDBUCK

Two species of reedbuck occur in the sub-region. The considerably larger reedbuck inhabits grasslands and the smaller mountain reedbuck is found on mountains or rocky hills. They are named for their characteristic association with the reedbeds of vleis and pans and with tall grass.

Reedbuck

Redunca arundinum

Rietbok

84

These medium to large antelopes vary in colour from brown, through shades of brownish-grey to greyish-yellow. The front of the forelegs is dark-brown. The grading of their colouration seems to nullify the three-dimensional shape of the animals and, taken together with their habit of 'freezing' in the event of danger, provides excellent camouflage. Only males have horns and these are forward pointing. The bases of the horns have a soft, bulbous, conspicuously shiny white swelling. There is a black, hairless glandular patch near the base of the ear, which appears to be more developed in animals in some areas, such as in Kruger national park, and even absent, as in animals from Kyle national park in Zimbabwe. Their voice in alarm, self-expression or territorial establishment, is a sharp clicking sound, caused by forced expulsion of breath through the nostrils, varying in pitch and tone. In distress the voice is a long-drawn plaintive cry and a soft hissing sound when suddenly frightened.

When they take flight they leap up and simultaneously jerk the hind legs, which movement is accompanied by a strange popping sound, believed to be the result of the sudden opening of the inguinal pouches. When pursued, they gallop very quickly and also stot with the hind legs pulled up towards the body, the hindquarters thrown high and the head erect, which exhibits the white throat-patch.

They are not gregarious and move about in pairs or small family parties. Temporary groupings occur during cold, dry months but are short lived. They move independently, but maintain contact by various means. Males defend their territories, chasing off any intruder to prevent them mating with

REEDBUCK

Gestation period: ± 230 days	
Young: one, sometimes two	
Mass: ♂ 80 kg, ♀ 70 kg.	
Shoulder height: ♂ 90 cm, ♀ 80 cm.	
Horns: 40 cm.	
Life expectancy: 10 years	

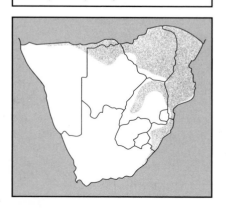

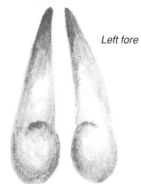

Left fore

³/₄ *actual size*

Left hind

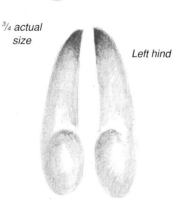

their females. They proclaim their territories by a proud, characteristic rocking canter, which conspicuously displays their white throat-patch.

Enemies are few as their traditional larger predators, such as lion, leopard and caracal are now rare in their range. One, sometimes two active young are produced.

Food: They are exclusively grazers, but in times of shortage they will resort to herbs and may browse extensively. They prefer to be near water.

Locally common in certain areas

Distribution: SOUTH AFRICA: *Transvaal*: Ben Alberts, Ben Lavin, Borokalano, Doorndraai Dam, Hans Merensky, Hans Strydom Dam, Klaserie, Kruger Park, Langjan, Lapalala, Londolozi, Loskop Dam, Mala Mala, Manyeleti, Nylsvley, Ohrigstad Dam, Pilanesberg, Rustenburg, Sabi-Sabi, Sabi-Sand, Suikerbosrand, Timbavati, Umbabat/Motswari; *O.F.S.*: Willem Pretorius; *Natal*: False Bay, Giants Castle, Hluhluwe, Itala, Kamberg, Loteni, Mkuzi, Ndumu, Phinda, Royal Natal, St Lucia, Umfolozi, Weenen; *Cape*: Amalinda, Botsalano, Mkambati.

SWAZILAND: Pongola; BOTSWANA: Chobe, Moremi; NAMIBIA: Eastern & Western Caprivi, Kaudom, Mahonga, Waterberg Plateau; ZIMBABWE: Chete, Chewore, Chizarira, Gonarhezhou, Hwange, Malapati, Mana Pools, Matopos, Matusadona, Nyanga; MOZAMBIQUE: Gorongosa, Maputo Elephant.

Mountain reedbuck
Redunca fulvorufula
Rooiribbok

85

This medium to small antelope is overall greyish to greyish brown, with upper parts of the tail and the head more reddish brown. The underparts of the body and tail are pure white. The coat is soft and woolly. Unlike the reedbuck, the front of the forelegs is not dark brown. The conspicuous black, hairless glandular patch below the ear is characteristic. Only males carry horns which are short, stout and forward curved.

They are gregarious animals, forming small herds of up to 30 but are more often encountered in groups of three to six. The groupings consist of territorial and non-territorial males, groups of females with young, and bachelor groups. Their alarm call is a shrill whistle, which sends the herd running away with tails held high. Territorial males remain in the territories throughout the year, leaving only for necessary grazing. If driven out, they will return. They will tolerate young males up to the age of about six months in their territories, thereafter driving them out, when the juveniles will join the bachelor herds.

Their preferred habitats are rocky hills, steep river banks and the slopes

MOUNTAIN REEDBUCK

Gestation period: ± 230 days	
Young: one	
Mass: ♂ 30 kg, ♀ 25 kg.	
Shoulder height: 73 cm.	
Horns: 32 cm.	
Life expectancy: 10 years	

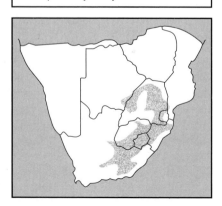

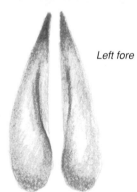

Left fore

Actual size

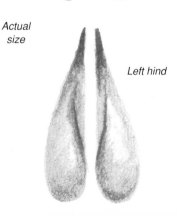

Left hind

Fairly common in
restricted areas

and terraces, rather than the summits, of hills and mountains. They are not equipped for the cliff-like steep places which suit the klipspringer. Bush and tree cover is essential.

They are generally diurnal but will move out onto the flats at night to graze or to drink.

Enemies are lion, cheetah, leopard and hunting dog. The young are preyed on by caracal, serval, baboon, jackal and large raptors. A single lamb is produced.

Food: They are exclusively grazers, taking only the softest new growth, avoiding the stems of the grass.

Distribution: SOUTH AFRICA: *Transvaal*: Ben Alberts, Borokalano, Doorndraai Dam, Hans Strydom Dam, Kruger Park, Lapalala, Loskop Dam, Nylsvley, Ohrigstad Dam, Percy Fyfe, Pilanesberg, Rustenburg, Sterkspruit, Suikerbosrand; *O.F.S.*: Erfenis Dam, Golden Gate, Hendrik Verwoerd Dam, Maria Maroka, Tussen-die-Riviere, Willem Pretorius; *Natal*: Giants Castle, Hluhluwe, Kamberg, Loteni, Mkuzi, Phinda, Royal Natal, Umfolozi, Weenen; *Cape*: Bontebok, Doornkloof, Karoo, Kommandodrift, Mountain Zebra, Oviston, Rolfontein, Thomas Baines, Zuurberg; SWAZILAND: Pongola.

✓ Waterbuck
Kobus ellipsiprymnus
Waterbok

86

These are large animals, which are seldom found far from water. They are somewhat docile, gregarious animals occurring in herds of about 6 to 12 animals, but sometimes they aggregate up to 30. They particularly favour riparian bush, where these donkey-like animals spend their rather sedentary lives, generally untroubled by predators, because of their unpleasant flavour. Sweat glands, most abundant on the flanks, but also distributed over the whole body, provide a dark waterproofing, musky, goat-like smelling secretion over the coat, which taints the flesh with which it comes in contact. For this reason, unless food is very scarce, they are generally shunned by the large predators, including even crocodiles.

They are readily identified by the white ring around their rear. There is also a whorl in the coarse shaggy hair in the middle of the back. In middle East Africa, the entire ring is solid white. Only males carry the heavily annulated horns.

Territorial males assert their position to strange males by a proud, intimidatory sideways display, which shows off the thickness of their necks. This display usually results in the departure of the stranger. However, should

WATERBUCK

Gestation period: ± 280 days	
Young: one, rarely two	
Mass: ♂ 260 kg, ♀ 230 kg.	
Shoulder height: ♂ 170 cm, ♀ 130 cm.	
Horns: 95 cm.	
Life expectancy: 17 years	

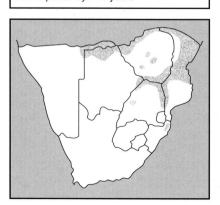

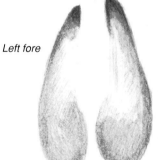

Left fore

½ actual size

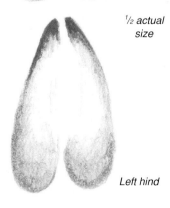

Left hind

this not succeed, then fierce fights occur which, more often than with other ungulates, result in the death of one of the combatants.

Voice is not often heard, except in rut, when the male 'snores' in sexual excitement. The female will utter a soft 'muh' if alarmed, calves reply with a high bleating.

Enemies are lion, leopard, hunting dog. Where game is not scarce, they are shunned because of their tough, stringy and strong-smelling flesh. One precocial young is born and rarely twins.

Food: They are predominantly grazers, but do also browse.

Distribution: SOUTH AFRICA: *Transvaal*: Ben Alberts, Ben Lavin, Blyde River Canyon, Borokalano, Doorndraai Dam, Hans Merensky, Hans Strydom Dam, Klaserie, Kruger Park, Langjan, Lapalala, Londolozi, Loskop Dam, Mala Mala, Manyeleti, Messina, Nyala Ranch, Nylsvley, Percy Fyfe, Pilanesberg, Roodeplaat Dam, Rustenburg, Sabi-Sabi, Sabi-Sand, Timbavati, Umbabat/Motswari; *Natal*: False Bay, Hluhluwe, Itala, Mkuzi, Phinda, St Lucia, Umfolozi.

Common in suitable habitat

NAMIBIA: Eastern & Western Caprivi, Mahonga; BOTSWANA: Chobe, Mashatu; ZIMBABWE: Chete, Chewore, Chizarira, Gonarhezhou, Hwange, Malapati, Mana Pools, Matopos, Matusadona, Nyanga; MOZAMBIQUE: Gorongosa.

Red lechwe
Kobus leche
Rooi-lechwe

87

The colloquial Tswana name 'leche' has given this animal its name. This water-loving animal ranks only with the sitatunga in its love of water habitat and, for this reason, its occurrence is discontinuous over its limited southern and central African range. It is an inhabitant of shallowly inundated, swamp fringes and rivers. It never strays far from permanent water, but differs from the sitatunga by utilising more open ecotone and shallower water. They have distinctly elongated hooves to aid in crossing muddy areas, but not approaching the extraordinary hooves of the sitatunga. Their distinguishing feature is the black line down the forelegs. They have lyrate, back-swept horns, which are carried only by males.

They are generally diurnal, but, where persecuted by hunting, they have become entirely nocturnal. They are adept swimmers and will not hesitate to take to water if in flight or to get at the aquatic grasses and other plants upon which they feed. They are gregarious, forming herds of 15 to 20 animals. Sometimes large aggregations form, but these are severely reduced from early days, when they numbered many thousands. A feature of the groups

RED LECHWE

Gestation period: ± 230 days	
Young: one	
Mass: ♂ 115 kg, ♀ 75 kg.	
Shoulder height: ♂ 100 cm, ♀ 95 cm.	
Horns: 85 cm.	
Life expectancy: 15 years	

Left fore

Left hind

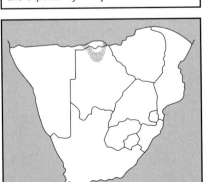

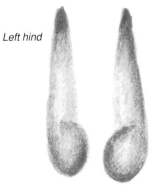

$^1/_2$ *actual size*

before the rut are the large bachelor herds which also include juvenile females.

They are territorial animals and a dominant male will gather its own herd of 10, up to 30, females. Territorial males permit sexually inactive males into their territory, but any show of sexuality causes the dominant male to present a show of aggression to displace that male. This rarely involves fighting.

If there are many males present which may pose a threat an intense display ritual of low horn sweeping takes place, often resulting in the horns being festooned with grass. Fights may occur in this case and these may be serious. The powerful swings of the vicious horns sometimes cause serious injury or even death. Voice is a series of whistles, coughs or grunts. The male will snort if suddenly disturbed, and calves bleat.

When pursued they scatter in small groups to the shelter of reeds and water. Their enemies are lion, leopard, cheetah, spotted hyaena, crocodile and python. Calves are eaten also by eagles. One precocial calf is produced.

Food: Grass and plants, including aquatic weed and grasses.

Distribution: NAMIBIA: Eastern & Western Caprivi, Mahonga; BOTSWANA: Chobe, Moremi.

Puku
Kobus vardoni
Poekoe

88

The name puku is supposed to have been given to the animal by David Livingstone from the name 'poku' by the local tribe. These medium-sized antelope, known elsewhere also as kob, are gregarious, occurring in troops of 2 to 40 animals and sometimes, rarely, up to 50. Bachelor herds occur and number up to 40 individuals. During the breeding season the herds are controlled by territorial males. They tend to have territories in more open areas which sometimes overlap the territories of other puku. When confronting a trespassing male, they wag their tails rapidly and sometimes clash horns, followed by chasing them off. This is usually sufficient to settle matters.

They are distinguished from the lechwe by the absence of the black bands down the front of the legs, are slightly smaller and are more brightly coloured. Their horns, which are carried only by the males, are significantly smaller.

Their activity is during the cooler parts of the day and into evening, the habitat being the zone extending from the edge of riparian and swamp-

PUKU

Gestation period: ± 265 days	
Young: one	
Mass: ♂ 75 kg, ♀ 60 kg.	
Shoulder height: ♂ 80 cm, ♀ 75 cm.	
Horns: 50 cm.	
Life expectancy: unknown	

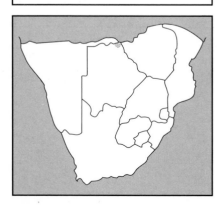

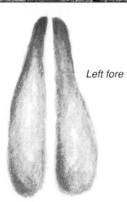

Left fore

½ actual size

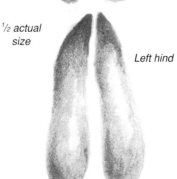

Left hind

fringe trees to the more grassy, drier areas, whereas the lechwe is intermediate between their range and that of the sitatunga, which are the true
swamp dwellers. Puku are relatively quiet, the males making a whistling
grunt when excited and the young bleating loudly when alarmed.

Enemies are, in particular, lion which penetrate the swamplands in
pursuit of sitatunga, lechwe and puku, also leopards, spotted hyaena and
hunting dogs. Servals and jackal prey on the young. One precocial calf is
produced.

Food: They are almost exclusively grazers, feeding on semi-aquatic grasses
and the grasses of the floodplains.

Distribution: NAMIBIA: Eastern & Western Caprivi; BOTSWANA: Chobe.

External Anatomy Terminology

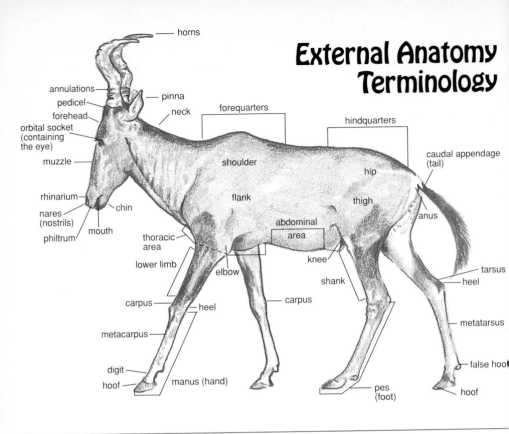

horns

annulations
pedicel
forehead
orbital socket
(containing
the eye)
muzzle

pinna
neck
forequarters
shoulder
hindquarters
hip
caudal appendage
(tail)

rhinarium
nares
(nostrils)
philtrum
chin
mouth
flank
thigh
anus

abdominal
area

thoracic
area
lower limb
elbow
knee
tarsus
heel

shank

carpus
carpus

heel

metacarpus
metatarsus

digit
hoof
manus (hand)
false hoof

pes
(foot)
hoof

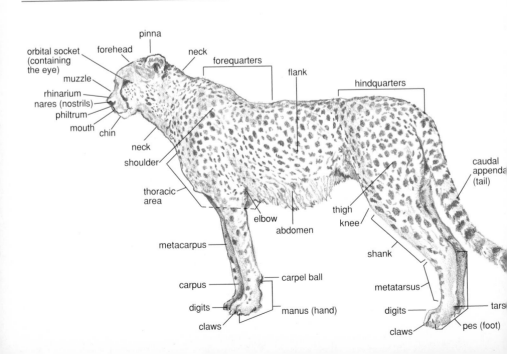

pinna

orbital socket
(containing
the eye)
forehead
muzzle
rhinarium
nares (nostrils)
philtrum
mouth
chin
neck
forequarters
flank
hindquarters

neck
shoulder
thoracic
area
elbow
abdomen
thigh
knee
caudal
appenda
(tail)

metacarpus
shank

carpus
carpel ball
metatarsus

digits
manus (hand)
digits
tars

claws
claws
pes (foot)

Glossary

Terms used in the study of mammals.

Albinism
Deficient pigmentation, characterised by a white and pinkish appearance, caused by a lack of melanin pigmentation.

Altricial
Helpless at birth, usually blind, with closed ears and partially naked. Requiring care.

Annulated
Ringed.

Anterior
At the front.

Antorbital
Situated at the front of the eye socket, or orbit.

Aquatic
Living in or near water.

Arboreal
Tree dwelling.

Bipedal
Movement on two feet.

Callosites
Thickened and hardened area of skin.

Canines
The teeth immediately posterior to the incisors.

Carrion
Flesh of a dead animal.

Carnassial teeth
Blade-like fourth upper pre-molars and first pre-molars, used for shearing through tough hide and meat.

Carnivorous
Meat-eating.

Caudal
Referring to the tail.

Carpus
Joints in an animal's wrist.

Caudal appendage
Tail

Copraphagy
The practise of eating dung to replenish micro-bacterium in the gut.

Crepuscular
Active around sunrise and sunset.

Digit
The finger or toe of an animal.

Digitigrade
Walking with only the digits on the ground (example cats).

Diurnal
Active during the day.

Dorsal
Referring to the back.

Ecosystem
A natural area which includes non-living substances and living organisms which interact to produce an interchange of material between the living and non-living constituents.

Ectoparasites
Parasites existing on the exterior of a host.

Endoparasites
Parasites existing in the interior of a host.

Exotic
Pertaining to introduced species.

Extant
Still in existence not extinct.

Falcate
Curved as a sickle.

False hoof
Shortened digits protruding at the back of the legs.

Fecund
Fertile.

Feral
Escapee from domestication or an introduced species which has reverted to a wild state.

Foraging
Searching for food.

Fossorial
Adapted to underground existence.

Frugivorous
Fruit-eating.

Genus (pl. genera)
Taxonomic classification category above species level.

Gestation period
The period between conception and birth.

Geophagia
The eating of soil by some herbivores.

Gregarious
Colonial living or other type of assemblage.

Habitat
A vegetation or climatic type in which a given type of animal has its being.

Herbivorous
Plant-eating.

Home range
The area over which an animal usually travels in pursuit of its normal activities.

Incisors
The most forward teeth in the jaw sharp-edged usually in the upper and lower jaw.

Inguinal
Situated in the groin i.e. the area between the lower lateral part of the abdomen and the thigh.

Insectivorous
Insect-eating.

Labial
Pertaining to the lips.

Lanceolate
Literally 'lance-shaped'.

Mandible
The lower jaw.

Manus
Entire hand section of an animal.

Maxilla
The upper jawbone which carries the upper canines and the cheekteeth.

Melanism
Abnormal development of darkening matter (melanin) in the skin.

Metacarpus
Part of the pes from the heel carpus to the joints of the digits.

Metatarsus
Part of the manus from the heel tarsus to the joints of the digits.

Molars
The grinding teeth, the most posterior cheekteeth.

Montane
Of mountainous terrain.

Muzzle
The part of the face which is anterior to the eyes.

Nares
Nostrils.

Oestrus
The period during which a female animal will mate for procreative purposes.

Omnivorous
Eating both animal and plant food.

Orbit
One of the two cavities in the skull containing the eye.

Orbital cavity
The bony socket enclosing and protecting the eyeball in the skull.

Parturition
The act of giving birth.

Phlanges
Digits.

Pectoral
Pertaining to the chest.

Pedicel
The bony raised platforms on which the horns of some antelope are mounted.

Pedal glands
Glands located in the feet opening between the hooves.

Pelage
The hair or woollen coat of an animal.

Pes
Entire foot section of an animal.

Philtrum
The narrow extension of the rhinarium joining the mouth.

Philoerection
Erection of the hair when under stress.

Pinna (pl. pinnae)
Ears

Plantigrade
Walking with entire foot on the ground (example man; rats).

Posterior
Referring to the back.

Postorbital
Posterior to the eye socket.

Precocial
Born in an advanced state of development, with all faculties developed and able to look after itself.

Prehensile
Able to be used to grasp.

Premolars
Teeth situated between the molars

and canines, preceded by milk teeth.

Preorbital
Anterior to the eye socket.

Rhinarium
The naked fleshy region at the tip of the muzzle which surrounds the nostrils.

Riparian or Riverine
Existence on the banks of rivers and streams.

Rostrum
The region anterior to the eyes, the upper muzzle.

Rugose
Corrugated, or wrinkled.

Scrotum
The pouch containing the testes.

Species (pl. species)
Taxonomic rank immediately below genus, also means actual or potentially interbreeding populations at a given point in time.

Subterranean
Existing underground.

Symbiosis
The mutually beneficial association between organisms, often necessary for survival.

Sympatric
Having the same or overlapping geographical distribution.

Tarsus
Joints in an animal's ankle.

Taxonomy
The classification and the naming of organisms.

Thermoregulation
The ability to regulate body temperature under different ambient temperatures.

Thoracic
Referring to the chest.

Ungulates
Hoofed animals.

Unguligrade
Walking only on the tip or the nail (hoof) of the foot (example antelope, horse).

Ventral
Referring to the underside or abdomen.

Bibliography

Child, G. *Behaviour of Large Mammals during the Formation of Lake Kariba,* Kariba Studies, Trustees of the National Museums of Rhodesia 1968.

Cillié, B. *A Field Guide to the Mammals of Southern Africa,* Frandsen Publishers, Sandton 1987.

de V. Pienaar, U., Joubert, S.C.J., Hall-Martin, A., de Graaff, G., Rautenbach, I.L. *Field Guide to the Mammals of the Kruger National Park:* Struik Publishers, Cape Town 1987.

Duthie, A. G. *The Ecology of the Riverine Rabbit Bunolagus monticularis.* Unpublished thesis, University of Pretoria, March 1989.

Haltenorth, Theodor, Diller, Helmut, *A Field Guide to the Mammals of Africa:* Collins, London 1984, 1986.

Liebenberg, L. *A Field Guide to the Animal Tracks of Southern Africa:* David Philip Publishers, Cape Town 1990.

Rautenbach, I.L. *Mammals of the Transvaal,* Ecoplan Monograph No.1: Ecoplan Pretoria 1982.

Smithers, Reay H.N., and Wilson V.J. *Checklist and Atlas of the Mammals of Zimbabwe Rhodesia,* Museum Memoir No 9, Trustees of the National Museums and Monuments, Salisbury, Zimbabwe/Rhodesia 1979.

Smithers, Reay H.N. *The Mammals of the Southern African Sub-region,* University of Pretoria 1983.

Stuart, Chris & Tilde, *Field Guide to the mammals of Southern Africa,* Struik Publishers, Cape Town 1988.

Photographic Credits

Daryl Balfour/ABPL: page 136

Anthony Bannister/APBL: back cover, pages 32, 34, 36, 39, 40, 50, 54, 56, 64, 69, 77, 81, 90, 98, 109, 111, 120, 122, 133, 138, 146, 148, 168, 172, 174, 176, 182, 185, 194, 196, 213

Daphne Carew/ABPL: pages 163, 212

Terry Carew/ABPL: page 142

Nigel Dennis/ABPL: pages 66, 156, 170, 172, 220

Richard du Toit/ABPL: page 96

Andrew Duthie: page 52

David Frandsen: title page, page 224

Clem Haagner/ABPL: pages 10, 14, 43, 87, 92, 94, 104, 116, 124, 129, 141, 144, 151, 160, 186, 190, 205, 211, 216, 222

Lex Hes: pages 45, 70, 74, 118, 136

Tim Liversedge/ABPL: pages 198, 207

Nico Myburgh: pages 59, 70, 107, 111, 112, 114, 153, 200, 209

National Parks Board: pages 48, 78, 84, 85, 102, 126, 162, 188

Robert Nunnington/ABPL: page 201

Peter Pickford/ABPL: pages 157, 203

Anup Shah/ABPL: front cover

Lorna Stanton: pages 100, 178, 192

Lorna Stanton/ABPL: pages 61, 76, 165, 218

Petri Viljoen: page 180

The spoor illustrations have been based largely upon the spoor illustrations in Louis Liebenberg's book, *A Field Guide to the Animal Tracks of Southern Africa*, published by David Philip Publishers, Cape Town.

Index